STAINED GLASS PAINTING ❧ Basic Techniques of the Craft

STAINED GLASS
PAINTING ✠ Basic
Techniques
of the
Craft

ANITA and SEYMOUR ISENBERG
RICHARD MILLARD

CHILTON BOOK COMPANY Radnor, Pennsylvania

We are grateful to Dorothy Maddy, who executed the Hebrew lettering shown in the color section, and to Mr. and Mrs. Howard Berkeley for allowing us to photograph Anita Isenberg's windows in their collection. One is shown on the front cover, and another in the color section. Our special thanks to Frank Reusche of L. Reusche & Co. for supplying much of the technical information on the manufacture of paints and stains.

Front cover: Window with painted details. *Anita Isenberg. Courtesy of Mr. and Mrs. Howard Berkeley.* Back cover: Two heads, with trace and matt. *Joep Nicolas. Courtesy of Richard Millard.*

Copyright © 1979 by
Anita Isenberg, Seymour Isenberg, and Richard Millard
All rights reserved
Published in Radnor, Pennsylvania, by Chilton Book Company
and simultaneously in Don Mills, Ontario, Canada,
by Thomas Nelson & Sons, Ltd.
Library of Congress Catalog Card No. 78-21826
ISBN 0-8019-6650-7
ISBN 0-8019-6651-1 (pbk.)
Designed by William E. Lickfield
Manufactured in the United States of America

2 3 4 5 6 7 8 9 0   8 7 6 5 4 3 2 1 0 9

To
TIFFANY, KENT, and CHRISTOPHER
A dubious troika

Like most poor rogues who live by their wits, we glass-painters have had our ups and downs. In one century petted by kings and mitred abbots; in the next utterly disregarded, or, worse still, hanged for idle rascals. It is with mixed emotions that one studies the history of his art. . . .

*   *   *

Sir: This day I have sent to you a box full of old stained and painted glass as you desired me to do, which I hope will suit your purpose. It is the best I can get at present. But I expect to beat to pieces a great deal very soon as it is of no use to me and we do it for the lead. If you want any more of the same sort you may have what there is, if it will pay for taking out, as it is a deal of trouble to what beating it to pieces is. . . .

MAURICE DRAKE
A History of English Glass Painting

❧CONTENTS

PART ONE

History, Tools, and Materials

ℳ CHAPTER 1

A Most
Mysterious Art

Of all stained glass procedures, glass painting has remained the most mysterious. This is the case not only for the beginning worker in stained glass, but for many who have been involved with the craft for years. Part of the problem is the lack of information available. Even worse is the amount of misinformation that is offered by so-called authorities or that has just grown up around the procedure. Much of this is so inhibiting to further efforts that many novices decide it's best to let glass painting alone. As a result, painting on glass has developed a mystical quality that appears to put it quite out of the reach of ordinary workers in the field.

Yet painting on glass is no more difficult or mystical than any other glass procedure. It is, in fact, the logical extension of one's familiarity with such glass craft procedures as cutting, leading and designing. Why not painting next? This is not to say you cannot learn to paint on glass if you haven't learned to cut and lead it. It is our view, however, that glass painting is not an end of itself. It is a part of the total experience of working with glass. It is a tool, not a goal. Glass painting, as we perceive it, is subordinate to and supportive of an additive glassy effect. It is not simply using a piece of glass for a piece of canvas.

The Purpose of Painting on Glass

Why bother to paint on glass, anyway? The glass we are discussing is, after all, already colored. It has been so treated in the factory by the addition to it in its molten state of certain metallic oxides. Cobalt will turn it blue, iron will turn it green, and so on. What particular purpose does it serve, therefore, to add more colors of paint to it?

The answer, of course, is—no purpose whatsoever.

And, having said that, let us clear up one of the basic confusions about glass painting as it applies to stained glass. We depend for our colors on the glass itself. The purpose of applying paint over these hues is threefold:

1. To control light more effectively. To make certain areas opaque—from the delicate details of a facial expression, to the blocking out of larger areas in order to direct the light precisely through a certain portion of the glass. In doing this we save a lead

3

line (to say nothing of a lot of fancy glazing) since we don't have to cut and fit another piece of glass.

2. To produce variety in degrees of translucency of glass. Paint allows us not only to control the light in sudden fits and starts, as from opaque to clear, but, depending on its application, to devise a blending over the glass surface that almost serves to slow down the light passing through it. Again, a semi-opaque glass might be substituted for the paint, but where will you find a glass that can modify portions of its opacity at your bidding? This can occur only through modification with paint.

3. To produce texturing of the glass surface. We will have a lot more to say about this in the chapter on diapering. Suffice it here to note that a painted surface can be given dimension with a brush or crumpled newspaper to produce striking and individual statements.

Painting on stained glass, therefore, requires a different way of thinking when compared to painting on canvas. It has been classified as "negative" canvas painting. Watercolor or oil painting involves reflected light and the putting in of shadows, values, and colors. Glass painting deals with transmitted light, light transitions, and the taking out of highlights. A good part of your rapport with glass painting will depend on how quickly you adapt to this new way of thinking.

Remember, a painting on canvas is not meant to enhance the canvas. It utilizes the canvas as a practical necessity. But the whole purpose of painting on glass is to enhance the essential glassiness of the conception. It is therefore important that there be a balance between the glass and the paint. Paint is not meant to be used arbitrarily over the surface. As soon as the paint obliterates the character and quality of the glass, it is being misused.

In the average studio, painting on glass is most frequently employed for graphic delineation of facial features, drapery lines, flower parts, motifs, and so forth. Secondarily, it is used for modeling effects; that is, to show degrees of light and shadow. Such degrees can be abrupt, as in a direct transition between matt paint and naked glass, or gradual, as in blending from a thick to a thin matt within the same piece of leaded glass. The effects that can be produced are inexhaustible—provided you always keep in mind the obligations to and capacities of the media in which you are working.

A Definition

We think it would be good at the outset to separate the phrase *stained glass* from *painted glass*. Many old books use the two terms synonymously. Stained glass is glass which has been colored in the factory by the addition of various metallic oxides (as described in the next chapter). Painted glass is, for purposes of this book, stained glass to whose surface has been applied various specific paints, themselves of a glassy constituency. A glass painting could not be made by staining the glass, as we have defined the term. A glass painting may be accomplished without using stained

Fig. 1-1 Nude, by Dick Millard. Sometimes mere touches of paint will do more than a whole palette of colors. Here the lead lines form the graphic detail on plain window glass; the hair and shadowing is done with matt and obscuring white paint.

glass. It would then be composed entirely on "white" or "bare" or clear glass (window glass).

Painting on glass, as the term is used in this book, is a very specific endeavor. It encompasses tracing, matting, stick-lighting, diapering, staining, firing—in short, any activity that involves the application or removal of paint from a piece of stained glass. The paint that we speak of is, itself, quite specific. The basic paints and stains are used only in the stained glass craft and are mixtures of powdered glass along with other substances.

To many people just being introduced to this type of painting, it may seem rather limiting. It is hardly that. It is one of the most challenging and rewarding of arts. Keep in mind that the glass itself furnishes the color. The paint is used to modify, transcend, and mold this light and color to predetermined effects, almost as a sculptor will mold a piece of clay. In the end he will have wrought from the clay an effect dependent on the material, yet unique of itself. The same can be done with glass painting, wherein the paint serves to enhance the wonder of the medium, not intrude upon it.

One basic question constantly arises: Does one have to be an artist in order to learn to paint on glass? In this book we aren't attempting to teach anyone to be an artist—especially since we aren't sure just what an artist is. If someone claims to be an artist on the basis of painting a piece of glass, don't let that inhibit *you* from trying simply because you aren't "artistic." And if you want to

What Is an Artist?

think of yourself as an artist, we aren't going to stop you. We certainly don't want you thinking of yourself as an artist on the basis of reading this book. This book is meant to teach technique: a very specific approach to a very delightful subject. We mean to do this in an orderly, rational manner. When you are done working with this book, you may or may not consider yourself an artist, but you will have under your belt basic skills for painting on glass.

Your Previous Experience

Your previous experience is quite another matter from whether or not you are "artistic." We feel that one should not approach the painting technique without a grounding in the basics of stained glass; that is, in the processes of pattern cutting, glazing, designing, and soldering. As we said earlier, glass painting is a part of the whole stained glass scene, not a separate element. Also important is some drawing experience. Again, it is not necessary that you be an artist, but you should have some drawing skills or some knowledge of human anatomy. It is not our purpose to teach drawing in this book. However, you may certainly use this book with a guide to drawing on hand, if your experience in this field is limited.

Your ability to reproduce what is in this book is not the issue. What we want is for you to take the information from this book and apply it to your own creations. The painting techniques we will be teaching here are applicable to any part of the body, any type of figuration. Such procedures as shadowing, matting, tracing, stippling, and diapering are applicable to the painting of any subject, though of necessity we have had to select certain specific subjects to demonstrate them. One such subject is the human head. Almost all of the elements of painting appear in the representation of the human head. Once you learn the technique, you can practice it on other heads, on other parts of the body, and represent different positions and direction of lighting. Remember, the effects of basic anatomy and source of lighting do not change just because one is painting on glass, even though the lighting must undergo certain modifications because of this new medium.

At least one reason not to feel inhibited if you haven't had too much painting experience is that glass painting can prove, for some experienced oil and watercolorists, a rather different sort of bird. It may throw their prior knowledge into a cocked hat. Since most glass painting is the reverse of regular painting, many painters accustomed to painting on canvas have trouble painting on glass. Sometimes it is more difficult to unlearn what you already know than to come to a subject with no preconceived ideas.

Expense

Most of your expenses will be on a one-time-only basis. Brushes, mahl sticks, easels, and spatulas do not wear out readily and, presumably, you already have a supply of stained glass.

One item that occasionally causes distress financially is the kiln—but it certainly doesn't have to. Many people make the mistake of buying a fairly large ceramic kiln. It is not necessary. A small enameling kiln will do. First of all, painted glass is not heated to the same high temperatures as are ceramic pieces; more important, glass lies flat on a shelf so you don't need the height of a ceramic kiln. While flash kilns are best for painted glass work, we don't recommend you go to the expense of buying one unless you are opening a professional studio. Most individuals buy small electric kilns and these will certainly do an adequate job. Used kilns are often for sale in craft magazines and these can be picked up quite inexpensively. Even if you have to replace the elements, a used kiln is usually worth the price, especially since just about nothing else can go wrong with it.

One major difficulty with buying supplies for glass painting is finding a source. And once such a source is found, how do you pick out from the catalog the items necessary to do the best job for the price? This is especially a problem for beginners in the craft, but many experienced hands we've talked to have pretty much the same difficulty. They solve it by sticking to tried and true materials—an advantage that can be somewhat limited by a disdain of newer items which may do a better job. Most people tend to stay with methods they've been taught and tools they are used to, a philosophy which we are not against, provided it does not limit adaptability.

We are going to discuss, in appropriate places, the various tools necessary to work effectively in this craft, as well as the specific paints. Here, again, confusion exists, since many different types and colors of paints are available. Glass painting, as we use the term, is a very specific craft, and very specific items are required. Prices, unfortunately, rarely stay specific. However, by the time you finish this book, you will have a good idea as to how much money you want to spend on supplies. You can get by for under $20, or you can spend into the hundreds.

One compromise you should not make is to buy more material at cheaper quality than fewer, more expensive, and obviously better items. It is better to buy two good brushes than four fair ones. The two good ones will last longer and do a better job for you than the four. In glass painting, as in most other things, you get what you pay for. Unfortunately, no matter how much you pay, none of these items will do the job by themselves. *You* must guide them. So, before you rush out and buy everything at once (which we have seen happen more than once), gather your information step by step and match it gradually with the proper tools and materials. Otherwise, you will end up with a number of items you will not use and did not need in the first place.

Nomenclature: Uses and Abuses

Painting, like any other art technique, depends on your artistic sense and is limited by your own aesthetic judgment, knowledge, and dexterity. But, like many other specialized fields, it has its own terminology which, far from standardizing and simplifying, can quickly become inhibiting to creative endeavor. We are not enraptured by terminology. What is a bristle brush in one part of the country may be a scrub in another; what to one individual is a "light" to another is the entire window.

In the course of this book we are going to try to stick to simple names, especially where the brushes are concerned. A fancy name can make a brush seem more difficult to use than it actually is, or can make it seem that the brush can be used only for one particular purpose. The student then becomes inhibited from using it for anything else. We have attempted to classify brushes simply by their use: tracers, stipplers, blenders, etc. Such names as *rigger* and *deerfoot stippler* also describe specific brushes with specific functions. A deerfoot stippler, for instance, is shaped like a hoof. This particular configuration of the bristles gives it a better stippling effect. A rigger is so called because it "rigs" a line around a piece of china. The name comes from its use in china painting, not for anything it does in stained glass.

By no means is a brush limited strictly to the use implied by its name. A tracing brush doesn't have to be limited to tracing, nor a matting brush to matting. There is no reason you can't matt with a tracing brush should the occasion arise.

In glass painting the matt generally provides the shadowing, the range in values from light to dark; the trace paint the graphic detail. But these terms are not fixed. You can use matt as a trace paint, and you can use a tracing paint as a matt. It depends on the effect you want to produce. Using matt as a trace paint will provide, in some aspects, a more subtle shading of the line than an abrupt jump from trace paint to matt, or, more extreme, from trace paint to bare glass.

When used to cover large surfaces, matt can be used in a single or in multiple applications. For instance, you can matt over a piece of glass, take out your highlights from the matt, fire, and then rematt. This will provide you with a doubled matt in some areas and a light matt in those areas that were formerly bare glass highlights. Depending on the number of firings you decide to do, you can rematt and take out highlights each time.

You can also matt on the back side of the glass for effect, though this might not be done in a window since the matt would then be exposed to the ravages of weather. As an experiment, or for small decorative pieces that will not be face-to-face with Mother Nature, reverse matting does provide some interesting effects.

Fluidity is the watchword in glass painting, though for instruction purposes a certain classification of tools and procedures becomes necessary. We hope you will keep this in mind through the course of this book.

Keeping an Eye on Perspective

The essential character of stained glass painting is, in most instances, best appreciated from some distance. Looked at close up, the most effective head, one which provides a clear-cut statement from across the room, will of necessity break apart into its components, just as a photograph printed in a newspaper would break up into its original dots if looked at with a magnifying glass. The exception to this are Swiss panels intended to be viewed close up.

Keep in mind, therefore, that you are painting up close, but that what you paint must read well from much further off. Color itself varies with distance, and it is even more variable when modified with paint. It is important to keep testing the relative values you are applying, either as texture or as light and shade, not only in proximity, but from a ways back. You may place some very subtle shading and congratulate yourself on having caught the mood of the thing precisely. From where you sit, perhaps. Yet, from ten feet away you may find this delicate transition totally washed out. Instead of those ingenious halftones, you've got a sort of paste. Should this happen, don't be discouraged. It is correctable—first by practicing your perspective, stepping back to have a look, and secondly by a judicious use of matt.

As a rule of thumb, we feel the closer the viewing is to be, the more subtle the permitted contrasts. The greater the distance your statement will have to reach across, the more contrast is required to give it the necessary oomph. There is a difference in painting for a lightbox in someone's living room or a church clerestory or an auditorium mural window. Keep in mind where the piece is going to be placed. Its location will inevitably affect how you are going to paint it.

Remember, always, that you are working with light. And light is a giddy thing. View right on top of your work and it is easy enough to see the films of paint that are holding back the light. But from a distance, such films may be unable to do the job. Light expands as it comes through stippling and cross-hatching; it pours through all available openings and radiates so as to obscure the painted details and reduce them to a form of silhouette. That may not be what you had in mind. If you fire it at this stage without checking it, you may be in for a shock.

Glass painting is like no other type of painting. Only in glass painting does everything you do constantly vary according to the amount and character of light available. Fortunately, you can modify the light coming in. It is really only "pure" light that plays tricks. Dimming this light with even a thin under-matting will calm this turbulence and allow your work to look the same from varying distances. So while it is all right to keep your nose to the grindstone in general, in painting on glass, at least, it helps to occasionally move it a bit farther back. This will permit you to check that what you are doing will indeed have the effect you wish it to have from a reasonable viewing distance.

Your Own Creativity

There are always two or three ways to a particular goal. We don't want to sound arbitrary in promoting our own methods, but the techniques we will be describing have worked well for us. What we intend to do in this book is to offer guidelines which should work well for you. However, you must always decide, "Which is the right way for me?" The end result is really all that matters. We feel that if you follow the instructions in this book, your end result will come about more effectively and more efficiently. We base this notion on our own creative experiences as well as that gained from teaching students in the past.

This does not mean, however, that you cannot modify some of these guidelines to suit your individual preferences. But be careful. Don't try to take shortcuts. Glass painting is a discipline as well as an art. The practice we urge upon you is all important. Finger, wrist, and arm motions, both separate and in tandem, are essential to getting the ideas in your head onto the glass. Too many individuals settle for a sloppy job because they are in too much of a hurry to get on with the next project. It is not as easy to develop good habits as bad ones; the wrong way always seems the more reasonable.

Each project in this book is calculated to teach you something about the one to come as well. We aren't running a race. Take your time. We would suggest that each time you go to paint, you spend time reviewing what you did last time. Establish a sense of security with the tracing brush and practice a few lines each time before going on to more ornate things. Don't be discouraged if what you learned yesterday seems to have left you today. Like establishing finger sense on a piano, the knowledge in your arm will come and go, flicker and fade. But persevere and you will suddenly find your painting taking on a certain logic of movement, an established direction, that will never leave you. At that point you will realize that all the practice, all the effort was worth it.

At that point you will be on your way to becoming a glass painter.

CHAPTER 2

The Nature of Glass Paint

When we talk about glass paint we are obviously not talking about the stuff you get at the local hardware store or paint shop. We are describing a specific item which has been used for hundreds of years in a very specific fashion. All glass paint that we include in this book is fired paint. Nonfired paints are available, but their use is limited to window glass, or small graphic effects on stained glass. Creativity with them is also limited since they utilize a piece of glass as a canvas, and they do not enhance the inherent qualities of the medium. No stained glass painter uses nonfired paints for any lasting work, though they can be fun to fool around with. Their effect is transitory, especially compared to the fired paints which can last for centuries.

Another distinction should be made between true glass painter's paints and enamels. To the glass painter, enamels are essentially low-fire, less wear-resistant colored paints, used to alter the color of the glass. Glass paints, on the other hand, are high-fire, permanent paints used to control the light transmission, translucency, and texture of the glass, and to effect changes in the value of the already colored glass. We will have a bit more to say about enamels later in this chapter, but it is important from the start not to confuse them with glass paints per se.

How Glass Paint Is Made

Glass paint is composed of two substances, the vehicle and the coloring agent. The vehicle is glass. It is made the same way that glass is made, but with certain modifications. It is composed of red or white lead oxide, sand, boric acid, clay, alumina, sodium, and potassium—all originally in powder form. This basic substance is variable in content. Some vehicles have a higher lead content, which makes for a softer (lower firing) glass. A lower lead content makes the vehicle harder (higher firing). All these powders are mixed together and poured into a clay crucible which is then heated in a furnace to about 1800°F. The amount of heat is dependent on what type of color you will be adding to the vehicle. At 1800°F this mass of powder melts, fuses, and becomes a glass.

Let's stop here just for a moment to consider the word *glass*. Although most people think of glass as a specific thing, it is, in fact, a term as unspecific as is the word *liquid*—which is, in fact, what

11

glass happens to be. It is as unspecific as any solid—which it also happens to be. This peculiar substance, this liquid-solid glass, is in this paradoxical state because it does not crystallize. It remains, therefore, an amorphous material; it has no molecular rigidity. If you think of glass in those terms, you can conceive of it as not a specific thing but rather a general substance—something to work with to make special things *from*.

We have said that the addition of lead will make the glass softer. It also makes the glass more refractive to light so that as light passes through it, an extreme bending of the rays occurs and a spread of color, a prismlike effect, takes place. This is the beauty of leaded glass crystal. The addition of silica to glass will make it harder. Other materials will make it more acid or alkali resistant.

The composition of glass is infinitely variable. Most glass is rather amenable and will take into its substance just about anything you apply, changing its physical properties to some extent thereby. One of the things you can apply is color.

Well, then, here we are with a rather large amount of molten glass in a crucible. It is now in an obvious liquid state and it is very thick. In fact, the unique part of this particular liquid is its viscosity. It is so thick that the molecules cannot get together to form crystals, though their natural tendency is to do just this. In addition to crystallization being hampered by the viscosity of the glass, the liquid is now beginning to cool. As it cools, the molecules within it begin to freeze. By the time room temperature is reached, we have what is really a supercooled liquid, the state in which glass remains.

It is a difficult concept for many people to accept—that glass is really a liquid. Yet if you were to measure old windows you would find them thicker at the bottom than the top, due to the slow but inexorable flow of the glass downward. In many high school physics laboratories, to prove the liquidity of glass, a piece of glass tubing is clamped into a vice with the other end unsupported. In time the tube bends downward.

There are certain things that can be done to molten glass to make it crystallize, however. If molten glass is held at the correct temperature for a long enough period of time so the molecules can get together, the glass devitrifies. It becomes cloudy, loses its strength, and crystallizes. At this point, it is no longer transparent and is quite useless for our purposes. You can sometimes see this effect occurring on old glass windows. Some Revolutionary War windows have crystals growing like trees over their surfaces, branching hither and yon as the glass devitrifies. It's rather sad in a way, like a frost of old age blurring the clarity.

We do not want our molten glass to crystallize, so we let it cool gradually. If we were to take it as it cools and simply pour it out of the crucible, what we would have would be a large ball of glass. A solid glass glob is a very difficult thing to work with considering the hardness of the material. Therefore, in order to get this cooling mass into a workable shape, we pour the molten glob into water.

Naturally, once it hits water it cracks apart. The amount of water that is used depends on how much glass you intend to pour in. Enough water must be used to allow the glass to cool instantly and crack and fragment to as great a degree as possible. This broken-up material is called a frit.

A frit is glass that has been poured into water in molten state and cracked. Jewelry enamels are made in this fashion; the word *frit* in fact is much more common among jewelry makers than stained glass workers.

The frit state makes the glass much easier to manipulate. The frit is placed in a ball mill, which is essentially a large jar with stones inside it. If stones are not employed, a very dense porcelain material called barundum is used. Ball mills come in all sizes— anywhere from a pint jar to 800 gallons. The mill is filled about half full with stones—very special stones, incidentally, not just any stones you gather up in your backyard. The best are the very hard flint pebble stones from the English Channel. Barundum is some-times more convenient. These come in quite heavy little cylinders.

You put your frit, which at this stage resembles a very coarse gravel or small pebbles, into the jar, fill it with water, and place it on a mill which tumbles it about. The process is similar to polish-ing stones in a tumbler. Inside the milling jar, the barundum is beginning to pound against the frit and grind it down. Ball mills are very effective instruments in reducing particle size. However, it does take a while (anywhere from forty-eight to seventy-two hours) before you come out with a powder, the end result of the frit that entered. The reason it needs this amount of pounding over this length of time is the hardness of the glass frit.

There are machines other than a ball mill that will reduce par-ticle size. One is a colloid mill, although glass is not really meant to be used in it. We even know some workers who have taken an or-dinary garbage disposal unit from the kitchen sink and used it to grind down glass. You won't get powder out of it, of course, and you don't get much efficiency either, since the gap between the rotor and the stater is too close to control the glass pieces. How-ever, it's a good enough way to chop up the glass into splinters or small pebble shapes. In any event, a disposal would not work for frit because the pieces are too large to work their way into the small grinding area.

Special tanks exist for taking the frit down to correct particle size. Think of a twenty-gallon aluminum cooking pot and imagine it filled with the barundum cylinders with a vibrator at the bottom. The same effect is accomplished as with a ball mill, but much faster. With the increased speed and efficiency, however, the par-ticle size must be watched carefully so the resulting powder is not too fine. Too fine a powder will lead to a very poor grade of paint which will crack after firing, just as fine mud will crack as it dries out after a rain. So if you ever buy paint that consistantly forms cracks after it has been fired (assuming you have added the right amount of gum and not a surplus) you may find it is the paint company that is at fault, rather than your technique. It is a reasonable complaint and should be brought to their attention.

While such fine powder is not good for glass paints, it is sometimes used in china painting, especially in the formation of raised enamel ledges such as one sees on certain teapots. Even here, if you study the paint lines closely, you can sometimes see the cracks that occur with a powder this fine.

Paint particle size, at least in this country, is usually watched quite closely. The basic particle size is controlled by having it pass through certain sizes of mesh. The usual painting particle has to pass through a #325 mesh (325 holes to the inch). However, certain imported paints may not be so scrupulously watched and cracking of the fired line can occur with them.

Adding the Color

We have now followed our painting vehicle from the original materials to frit to powder. Next, the wet powder is dried by evaporating the water and you end up with a white substance resembling talcum powder (it may be yellowish if very high amounts of lead were used). This powder is called *flux*. Flux is a word used differently by different craftspeople. We use the word to denote something that causes something else to fire at a lower temperature. Interestingly enough, in ceramics, a flux for glazes which melts at 1700°F is a refractory (heat-resisting) agent for glass painting colors which generally fire at about 1200°F.

This "talcum powder" or flux is the base of the paint. We must now add a color to it, since so far the powder will form just a sort of milky film that will do nothing for anyone's aesthetic sensibilities. The flux acts almost as a catalyst as well as a vehicle. Think of this flux as a bridge between the coloring agent it is carrying and the glass surface it will help bind it to. It is in fact a matrix, a bonding as well as a carrying agent. What it carries and bonds is, of course, the color; that is the essential ingredient of the whole endeavor.

What is this color and where does it come from? In the Middle Ages and the Renaissance, glass painters made their colored glass a bit differently than we do today. They started by making a very soft (low-firing) glass and added specific coloring agents directly into it in the molten state. Any metallic oxide would serve: cobalt for blue, copper for green, manganese and iron and antimony—all would color the molten glass according to its disposition. Gold from gold coins was used to make a deep ruby color. Throwing such metallic oxides into the pot of molten glass would provide them with a colored glass that was transparent.

Some of these coloring methods are still used today. If you want to make some ruby glass, for example, try throwing a gold coin into some of your melted-down glassware. You will find, to your financial embarrassment, the glass will stay clear. However, if you then take this glass down to a somewhat lower temperature than before, throw in your gold coin and hold the temperature constant, you will be rewarded by seeing the glass turn ruby. This process is called "striking the color" and it was well known in the Middle

Ages. What happens is that the molten glass begins to grow a colloid of gold. (A colloid is a suspension of particles in a liquid that stay suspended—they do not settle out.) These particles are infinitesimally small. In fact, the smaller the particle size, the redder the color—a bit of natural economic husbandry which allows a small amount of gold to achieve a rich hue. As the particle size gets larger—if, for instance, too much gold is added for the amount of glass available—the color begins to move from red to maroon to blue.

This was how the old "pot metal" glass was made, but when it came to making a colored paint, these early painters found that they needed a medium that would hold the color to the already existing glass. What they were looking for, basically, were colors to block out the light. They weren't interested in transparent colors because they already had their transparent color in the glass.

What they utilized were substances such as umber (an iron oxide), oxides of manganese, or any of the earthy metallic oxides that were available to them. These they would grind up and mix with a frit (glass), the whole thing being mulled into a fine powder. When this was mixed with water it would flow over the glass surface, and, when fired, the frit would melt onto the glass surface and hold the color in place.

The manner in which the color for paint is made today is not quite the same. What is manufactured is a refractory oxide that does not melt. For instance, the glass or paint manufacturers will mix substances such as cobalt, chrome, clay, and alumina together with sand and fire it to 2600°F. At this point, all these elements fuse together (they do not melt, a different reaction entirely) and they form what is called a clinker. This is almost like an ash. The clinker is formed through a solid state reaction during which the cobalt and the chrome join together with the silica and form a spinnel, a chrome alumina silicate. This is now a very specific color. The one we are discussing is a black pigment which is insoluble in glass.

The manufacturer takes the clinker and grinds it into a powder. The two ingredients for paint are now side by side—on the one hand this black powder, on the other the flux powder from the frit. Mix both these items together and lo and behold you have a color. It isn't all quite that simple, of course (nothing is) but that is the idea. The kind of color you will have depends upon the ratio of color to flux. Be that as it may, the end result is a paint that you can now paint on glass with. A lot of the paint's integrity depends on how thoroughly the flux and color have been mixed. A number of methods are used for this. Some factories ball mill the two substances; others use a sonic mill, or they can be mixed by blending them through sieves.

The Importance of Lead

Lead oxide is a very important constituent of glass paint. It is one of the base elements, used not for color, but to make the flux fire at a lower temperature than it otherwise would. Naturally your glass paint has to melt at a lower temperature than the glass you are painting on. Routine painted glass firings occur at about 1100°F. If things get too hot, your cut glass pieces may show some shrinkage. Many glasses are fussy as to temperature, and it is important that you try to humor their little idiosyncrasies. Otherwise, you may find them coming out a different color than you had calculated. Rubies are notorious for this.

As we mentioned earlier, putting lead into glassware gives the glass a higher refractive index, which provides more sparkle to the finished product. The lead in the glass gives it this crystalline appearance. It also makes the glass more difficult for a glassblower to work with since it makes the glass fire at a much lower temperature and it can thus slump more readily. But adding lead is worth it to get this sparkling effect.

The simplest type of glass to deal with is the routine lime glass which is used for window panes. This has no lead added to it. You can take this glass and blow the most gorgeous article in the world from it—but it would look flat. Since it would have no refractive index, the light would simply pass straight through it. Pound for pound, of course, leaded glass is heavier than unleaded glass. Some of the most heavily leaded glass is found in the windows of x-ray booths. They are also extremely heavy in weight.

Lead also happens to be a glass former. There are few substances that will provide this strange noncrystalline material. Silica is, of course, another. Glass formers, because of the type of atoms of which they are composed, apparently fit into the glass network. Think of a piece of glass rather as a fish net. The lines of the fish net are composed of silica and oxygen in a sort of random pattern. (It has to be random; if the lines of the fish net formed a regular network, the glass would crystallize.) Like any fish net, the random lines form variously sized spaces or holes between them. Some elements will fit directly into the lines of the network itself. Silica, oxygen, lead, and boron are among this group. All form part of the network skeleton. Sodium, potassium, and calcium are elements that are found in the holes in the network. The ability of glass to take paint or a stain depends on how tight this network is and how amenable some of these "hole" elements, such as sodium, are to changing places with, say, the silver in a silver stain.

We will have more to say about this in the chapter on staining. Suffice it here to note that not all glass is the same. The individual peculiarities of a piece of glass depend on the tightness or looseness of the network, the amount of lead and the amount of silicate, to mention a couple of factors. You will find, as you pursue your painting career, just how frustrating it can be to spend a lot of time painting or staining a piece of glass that isn't in the mood. We make it a habit to test fire all glass that is new to us before getting to work on it. Other than finding out how readily it will accept such surface modifications, one gets an idea how stable the glass's own color is. Ambers, browns, and reds can develop schizophrenic tendencies at certain temperatures. There is little use in having your painting turn out perfectly when the color you've calculated it to goes up in smoke.

Enamels

You might logically ask why, since paint is really glass with pigment in it, you can't take a piece of glass which already has pigment in it (stained), grind it up, get a flux that will hold it to a piece of glass, and melt it on as a transparent enamel? Well, you probably could, although we've no first-hand experience with the method ourselves. It seems to be a bit like reinventing the wheel. Why go through all the work when the material is ready at hand? And, even though it sounds theoretically possible, there would still be a lot of trial and error to go through.

More to the point is the use of the word *enamel,* which is a word that is more bandied about than understood. It tends to mean different things to different people in different lines of work. For instance, what a china painter calls enamel is quite different from what a glass painter means by the word. To a glass painter, an enamel is a low-fire decorative color which tends to be transparent. It has much less resistance to weather or to detergents than do the high-fire paints, and far less than the glass stainer's stain. Putting enameled glass into a dishwasher will result in some loss of surface, and as the process is repeated, the enamel will eventually wear away.

There is little call for the development of a high-fire enamel paint for the stained glass industry, because glass painters are already dealing with the color in the glass and rarely need extraneous color to add to it. One instance, however, in which enamels are used in glass work is in the painting of Tiffany figures, especially Tiffany flesh (head, hands, feet, etc.). Such painting is more closely related to china painting than to glass painting. The Tiffany painters employ, generally, an obscuring white paint for background use. This is a basic ground for the Tiffany head style in particular. This base of obscuring white paint diffuses or obscures the light coming through the glass, thus forming a translucent backdrop. Other enamel colors are then added over this obscuring white to get the true Tiffany effect. A translucent glass of similar color does not give nearly the same blend as the paint which, after all, can be applied arbitrarily. Tiffany artists often double glaze glass behind their semi-transparent foreground glass.

A few of the Tiffany style painters we spoke to said they preferred painting over the obscuring white paint to using a piece of opaque glass as they got a better "bite" with their tracing brush from the more substantive surface furnished by the background paint. You will be able to judge this different feel of painting yourself when we get into the technique of tracing over unfired matt.

Sad to say, much of the exquisite painted craftsmanship of many Tiffany windows is already faded and worn—a tribute to the self-destructive element built into low-firing, impermanent enamel painting.

This does not mean that there is anything wrong with painting

with enamels, should you desire to try it. The Reusche catalogue
has a lot of enamel colors for you to choose from. As long as you
use clear glass (or lightly tinted if you prefer) to get the best effect,
and as long as you use these paints on something that will not be
exposed to the weather nor washed too often in the dishwasher,
you can come up with some interesting creations. However, once
again, you will be using the glass basically as a canvas, not so
much as an expressive modality in its own right.

Enamels are often used in a silk-screening process on glass,
which is still another technique that can be used to cover a glass
surface with paint. There are a number of adept practitioners of
this art around.

The Longevity of Glass Color

Is it possible that colors of antique glass actually change, or is
the apparent change of color in old windows simply a patina from
the weather over the years? We know the weather does add grit
and grime, to say nothing of the effects of exposure to sulphuric
acid. This has more of a debilitating action on the glazed, rather
than the painted, sections. The lead and putty, rather than the
glass, seem to be most affected.

But if colors actually do change, atmosphere must have something to do with it. Sulphuric acid can condense on glass surfaces
if there is sulphur dioxide in the air. This is a good thing to keep in
mind if you are painting a window that is in an area of high pollution. Examination of some of the windows of Chartres Cathedral
reveal a red color that, since it is not duplicated today, might be
due to ultraviolet rays from the sun acting on the original hue over
the centuries. However, this seems unlikely; more likely is that
this red color is still pretty close to the original. The fact that it is
not produced today does not mean it cannot be produced. It means
it is not worthwhile or economical to produce it for general avail-
ability.

Consider something else: there are only around twenty-three
colors all told in the Chartres windows—not very many compared
to the hundreds that we work with today. Almost all of these colors
seem to have undergone change; that is, they vary from what one
supposes was their original hue. But a lot of this supposed change
is illusory. Color tends to vary with the thickness of the glass,
which, of course, is hardly uniform in the Chartres windows. And
much of the effect of the Chartres windows must be attributed to
two other factors: the imposition of nature over the centuries giving them a quality that was not there originally, and the chance
impurities present in the various batches of pot metal glass used to
make the windows. What these impurities were and their percent-
ages, one cannot even imagine. But it is more likely that it is these
variables, rather than fading of the color due to sunlight, that have
provided the different tone combinations. Stained glass colors are
as permanent or fragile as the glass itself—a further paradox of
this most paradoxical material.

No introductory discussion of glass painting would be complete without at least one mention of a very special paint—Rouge Jean Cousine. Always in demand by glass painters, it happens to be a paint that you will most likely never use because you'll never be able to find it. Few are the glass painters who even have small samples of the stuff. One would almost be tempted to believe this fabulous material never existed, except for the obvious presence of windows containing glass that was painted with it.

We are fortunate enough to possess a painted piece done with Rouge Jean Cousine (see color section), and the effect is simply marvelous. It is a very special flesh tint which has a transparency that is unimpeded by any translucency. It is a sort of brownish-red color. When it is mixed with the vehicle (vinegar, water, or oil) it provides a versatile flesh color. Is there, as has been guessed, no more than perhaps ten ounces in the whole world?

What makes this stuff even more unusual as a paint is that this special reddish flesh tint is applied on the *back* surface of the glass, just as a stain would be. This implies certain stain qualities. It also appears to be impervious to weather—again a similarity to silver nitrate stain. Something seems to happen in its reaction with glass when it is heated; like silver nitrate stain, it possibly penetrates the glass.

What its formula is, is anybody's guess. One paint manufacturer told us he acquired a formula for Rouge Jean Cousine which had everything in it but bat's wings. The idea was to ball mill the material, make a very fine powder in a pot, and leave it in the sun to sit for six weeks or six months. After that time, he was to throw out whatever didn't turn brown. He calculated, with luck, he might have a slight residue at the bottom of the pot. Even at a $1,000 an ounce, it hardly seemed worthwhile.

We have located one or two painters who claim to have some Rouge Jean Cousine, but we were unable to get them to demonstrate it, much less part with any. So, if in your glass painting perambulations you stumble onto this material, don't think, "It's just another flesh tint; what do I need it for?" At the very least, you can call us.

Going from the sublime to the actual and real, there are some paints you will be using which we would like to mention at this time. The Reusche catalogue lists a great number of paints and many individuals find this array confusing. Many of the paints listed have nothing to do with glass painting; they are for china painting and have nothing to do with the subject of this book.

The glass stainer's paints fall into two main categories: those manufactured by Hancock and those by Drakenfeld. There are subtle differences between the two. The Hancock paints seem to have the best resistance to weather. However, the Hancock colors are more difficult to work with than the Drakenfeld, which are no slouches themselves when it comes to permanency. Hancock colors tend to be quite gritty and take a lot of grinding with muller and palette to get them to flow smoothly, whereas the Drakenfeld colors need only the usual mixing with the spatula.

We feel you should have experience with both types of paint and decide for yourself which one you want to make your staple colorant. Besides, we feel you should have the experience of grinding paint—a subject which will be taken up in the appropriate chapter—and you will certainly get that experience with Hancock. Neither the Hancock nor the Drakenfeld will come off the glass if fired correctly, and they both stand weathering well.

Another problem with Hancock colors is that they are not all uniform. The variation is slight, but it can make enough of a difference to be annoying. The intensity can vary. Some blacks go a little browner than others, some are darker than others. You can never be quite sure what you are going to get as a result. For the beginning painter it may not matter a whole lot, but when you are a professional trying to match an existing color, it can matter quite a lot.

Many older glass painters use Hancock paints almost exclusively since that is what they were trained on, and one tends to adhere to past security. They are quite adept with the material and take the requisite grinding for granted. Where Hancock paints do have a particular value is as additives in matching up colors for restoring old windows. Some painters who do a lot of restoration use Hancock colors themselves as coloring agents—adding them, say, to a Drakenfeld color to get a more intense or more dilute equivalent.

Other than the black tracing paint, you will be using flesh tones quite a lot in the course of your painting. There are some that are useful substitutes for Rouge Jean Cousine, though, of course, we're only saying that out of spite. Drakenfeld flesh red #476 is a fine flesh tone which is nicely semi-transparent. Drakenfeld #1326-A is also a good flesh tint. Hancock #1333 (Hancock Red for Flesh) is our choice.

We will be talking further about specific paints you should have on hand as we go along. The paints we will be mentioning are specific choices; please do not use others unless you are sure they are closely related. All the paints we will use are fired paints; unfired paints will not substitute. You won't need all that many paints for a start, and they are not expensive. In fact, for the effects you can produce with them and the satisfaction which we are sure you will gain, they are cheap at the price.

We suggest that you get some clean bottles and pour your powdered paints into them, labeling each bottle. Paints are purchased in paper envelopes which, as you go along, tend to fold, crease, and eventually develop leaks. As you accumulate paints, you will find it difficult to store these little envelopes and find just the one you want when you want it. It is much neater, cleaner, and more convenient to store paint in bottles. Keep a shelf or two just for your painting materials so they do not get mixed up with your other stained glass items.

Speaking of price, one good measurement to keep in mind, since paint is sold by the ounce, is that an ounce is about a full table-spoonful. This will give you a measurement to calculate with. To start off with, you shouldn't need more than a few ounces of the several paints that will be mentioned herein.

CHAPTER 3

Painting Styles and Characteristics

It is not our purpose in a book of this nature to provide a detailed background of glass painting. At the same time, for the student to understand much of what is done today, as well as the techniques employed, it would be well for him to have some sense of the history of the art.

Early English Style

Any classification of painting styles is arbitrary. The first, or Early English, lumps together all glass paintings before the year 1280. So you can see that glass painting goes back a long way. The oldest examples that can reasonably be dated seem to be those in

Fig. 3-1 Early English style. 12th and 13th centuries.

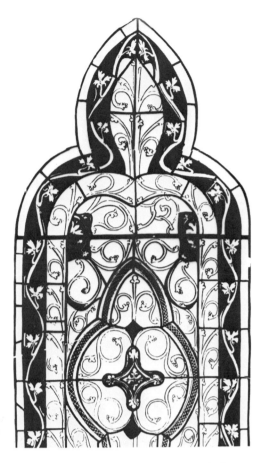

Fig. 3-2 Decorated Style.
14th century.

the abbey church of St. Denys in France which are dated about
the 1150s. Early English painted windows are almost entirely composed either of colored glass or of white glass, with the colored
glass windows devoted almost entirely to pictures and the white
ones to patterns. Both are usually surrounded by a wide colored
border. As shown in figure 3-1, the painted figurations are tall and
slender, somewhat out of proportion and stiff. Draperies are very
interesting, with a great many folds of cloth. Figured details are a
little disappointing, somewhat crudely drawn. The figures in these
windows tend to stand out from the background because they are
always much larger than the background, even disproportionately
so.

The so-called Decorated Style (figure 3-2) held sway from about
1280 to 1380. As its name indicates, its principal ingredient was a
particularly ornamental approach, specifically where natural ob-
jects were concerned. The painters of this style paid a lot of attention to leaves and foliage, representing them in a flowing, decorative way that contrasted with the plain, less dimensional painting
done before.

Borders, and especially heraldic borders, are common in this
style, as are repeated ornamental patterns against white glass.

Decorated Style

It was during the latter part of this period that silver stain came into use, providing the deep lemon color that is so flexible in its effects. It added an amount of gaity and charm to the rather stiff grandeur of the earlier Decorated Style, whose windows tended to be rather cold looking, due to the amount of white glass that was interspersed among the colored. Silver stain, once it was introduced, spread rapidly as a technique and was applied then, as today, on the back surface of the glass. Water, rather than vinegar, was the preferred vehicle and it was applied quite thick, one book advising a depth to $1/16$ inch.

Perpendicular Style

In the movie *Kind Hearts and Coronets,* Alec Guiness, as the old cleric taking his murderous guest on a tour of his church, points out the stained glass windows and mumbles with pride about their being "early perpendicular." Since he was early on to being horizontal, it seemed a delicate touch. A delicate touch indeed is characteristic of the Perpendicular Style (figure 3-3), which shows a minute attention to detail in the figurations, as well as subtle shadings and choice color sense. The ornamentation is equally finely executed. In short, the Perpendicular window is quite elaborate; so much so that many of these windows tend not to "read" well from a distance. This is an element of glass painting that we are going

Fig. 3-3 Perpendicular Style. 15th century.

Fig. 3-4 Cinque Cento
Style. Early 16th century.

to discuss further in succeeding chapters. A certain timidity of
outline seems also to be characteristic of many windows of the Perpendicular Style, with a lot of stipple and smear shading which,
again, we will get into in the chapter on matting.

Not much flesh-colored glass was used; some pink, but mostly
white, is what we meet with in this fifteenth-century technique.
Gradually the fleshy portions of the figures were colored with a
reddish tint, but this was more a sixteenth-century development,
though, of course, such developments were not isolated to particular times.

Shadowing—an effective use of light and dark—seems, however, to be primarily a sixteenth-century technique, and it is one
we use quite freely today. Such bold and abrupt transitions can
provide a strong sense of drama in a painting, specifically emphasizing the transmission of light through the glass. (Matting, as we
will point out again, gives a particularly "glassy" effect.) Wherever
necessary, shadowing was done on both sides of the glass in order
to increase the effect. Stippling was a necessary adjunct to shadowing then as it is today.

The "golden age of glass painting," at least according to one au-
thority, reached perfection in roughly the first half of the sixteenth
century during the Cinque Cento Style (figure 3-4). Characteristic
of this approach were fantastic displays of color, as well as abrupt
changes of light and shadow that still left the glass transparent.
Unfortunately, as painters of this school kept striving for a unique
effect, this transparency began to give way to coats of paint in
more strikingly shadowed arrangements. Gradually, as more and
more glass painters strove to imitate oil painters using canvas, the
glass lost its peculiar individuality.

All the same, glass painting at this time was not only being done
by master painters who had a strong sense of color values, but a

*Cinque Cento
Style*

certain achievement in the production of stained glass kept step
with this artistic advance. Many new tints of glass were being
made with, it seems, quite a number of "streakies" or "reamies."
Such flashes of color in the glass, bold or subtle, accidental or
planned, were taken advantage of by the painters of the day and
incorporated into their endeavors. It's something still to keep in
mind today, when the choice of glass has reached proportions that
can only be considered amazing when one looks back over a period
of just a few years. If you are constantly aware of the nature of the
material you are painting on, you'll be surprised how often it will
contribute its own personality to what you are imposing on its surface.

Intermediate Style

In the Intermediate Style (figure 3-5), enamel colors began to be
employed, following their discovery about the middle of the sixteenth century. These colorants are generally used only on white
(clear) glass since they are, in effect, colored paints. Enamels are
usually soft, low-firing paints, and they tend in time to fade and
deteriorate. However, some beautiful work can be done with
enamels, as witness certain of the Swiss Heraldic panels of this
period (figure 3-6).

Unfortunately, the temptation of early glass painters to fudge
with a piece of enamel-covered or partially covered clear to get out
of a difficult glazing procedure resulted in a mixture in some windows of stained glass and enameled glass pieces. You can easily
tell which is which if you see a piece of clear glass that suddenly
becomes colored partly across its surface. If it is entirely enameled,
it will look duller than the pot metal glass surrounding it. Enamels
were often used to heighten the tints of the stained glass pieces.
The problem was that here, once again, the glass was being used
as a canvas out of convenience and misunderstanding of the medium.

On the whole, it is as true today as it was then that mixing
enamel paints with "true" stained glass paints is a tricky business.
It may diminish the overall effect if it is overdone. The painters of
the Tiffany school show how enamels can be applied to enhance
the glass, and, indeed, the two types of paint, longevity aside, can
be combined in the hands of accomplished workers to stunning
purpose.

Fig. 3-5 Intermediate Style. Late 16th century.

Fig. 3-6 Swiss Heraldic panel. 16th century.

What caused the decline of painted glass in the seventeenth century has never been fully decided. Everybody has reasons of his own. Undoubtedly the politics of the time, which resulted in the smashing of a great number of windows in England and France, demeaned the craft. Wars and windows do not go well together. Possibly the arbitrary use of enamels contributed. In France, for example, where enamels did not get nearly the hold on the glass painter's fancy that they did in England, Holland, and Belgium, there was not the considerable decline in the art as was seen in those countries. Whatever the reason, at this time there seemed to be a steering away from glass as a medium to glass painting as an imitation of oil painting on canvas. For the purposes of our survey, the point can be taken that use of enamel paints on glass is quite a different thing than glass painting as such. While the two may be kissing cousins, a marriage should be contemplated only under special conditions.

Three Methods of Painting

From the above discussion it can be seen that three systems prevail in painting on glass. First is the mosaic method, in which pieces of colored or uncolored glass are jointed together like a picture puzzle, the main outline being formed by lead came which surrounds and connects the various pieces of glass together. Painting on these pieces is limited to what are called glass stainer's colors: trace pigment, matt colorants, and stain. The major color comes from the glass itself. Each color of the design must be represented by a separate piece of glass, though a limited number of colors can be shown on the same piece of glass through the processes of etching (aciding) or staining, or a combination of both. Two shades of yellow may be shown on one piece of glass by multiple staining. Other than that the rule holds: one color per piece of glass. (This excludes, of course, reamies or streakies which have multiple colors in the same glass piece but which for our purposes are considered as one color.)

The enamel method does not use colored glass, nor is it necessary that the glass be cut into a mosaic fashion. A single piece of glass can suffice since the colors are applied to the glass by the brush of the artist. It is not necessary to acquire color from the glass itself, so really no glass cutting is necessary at all. The glass is used as a transparent canvas. The application of color to glass in this fashion arose at a much later date than did "true" glass painting—about the middle of the sixteenth century—and quickly became widespread. In fact, by the eighteenth century this technique almost entirely superseded the use of colored glass painting in large works. Enamel painting tends to lose in transparency what it gains in variety of color and the ease in using a single piece of glass as a base, so it does not have the depth of color provided by true colored glass (Swiss glass paintings of the sixteenth and seventeenth centuries excepted).

The third method is a combination of the above two and is called the mosaic-enamel method. Here the window is put together in a mosaic fashion, and both enamels and glass stainer's colors are applied. Enamels may be used on areas of clear glass (as in Tiffany head or flesh painting) or even on colored glass to emphasize or subdue portions of these tones. The glass paints are used, as usual, for graphic detail and shadowing.

In this book we are concerned with the mosaic method. The techniques necessary to school oneself in glass painting are almost all to be found in this particular approach. Once these techniques are thoroughly learned, the craftsman will have a firm basis of control and can adapt them to any other style of painting.

Grisaille

Grisaille is not a painting style, but because it is often confused for one, we thought we would discuss it here. The word *grisaille* means "grey"—the implication is gray glass. Occasionally the term was applied to white (clear) glass. Neither white nor gray, grisaille really indicates a type of ornamental stained glass work, originating in the thirteenth century, that shows the bulk of the glass as white. Or clear. Or gray, due to painted detail over the surface. Interspersed with this lack of hue are some colored jewels, and there may be a colored border as well. That is true grisaille; there are, of course, modifications.

The most famous of all grisaille windows, and one of the most famous of all stained glass windows thanks to Dickens, is the Five Sisters at York, England. Contrary to its title, this is not a figured window, but five identical "lights" or panels, mosaic in design and delicately matted, with interludes of colored glass in rhythmic order.

We tend today to think of stained glass windows as full of colored glass, and the effectiveness of a window is calculated by these
calibrated tones. This was not the case with thirteenth-century
grisaille. Throughout most of the history of stained glass, clear
glass played a great part, interrupting the inexorable march of
color, conducting the tempo of the composition. Grisaille, however,
was an extreme example.

What the purpose was in colored glass suddenly being dropped
in this fashion no one really knows. From the gorgeous, intense
hues of the twelfth and early thirteenth centuries, all of a sudden
we have grisaille. A number of theories have been advanced for
this. Cheapness was one, since clear glass is, of course, less expensive than stained glass. Also, more light is available through clear
glass. Some researchers believe the reason was a religious one—a
wave of reformation in the church which saw in these luscious
tints, these resounding palettes of color a reflection of the opulence
and luxury indulged in by many of the church hierarchy.

Whatever the reason, a fine grisaille window need not take a
back seat because of its uncolored nature. The overpowering effect
of the Five Sisters, their sheer massiveness aside, is magnified by a
reverberation of light from the matted surfaces of the otherwise
clear glass.

CHAPTER 4

The Work Area and Necessary Materials

Glass painting does require certain specific materials as well as room. In this chapter we are going to tell you straight what you will need. How much individual items cost is difficult to say. Prices keep changing. If you are really interested, pick up a phone and call your paint supplier. Our purpose is not to tell you how much to spend, but how to save. You can save by not purchasing items for which you will have no immediate use; you can save by knowing what to buy so you do not overlap materials; you can save by making certain things yourself. Above all, you can save, next to money, the most important commodity: time. We will give you some of the shortcuts we have found that work well for people just starting to paint. If you already have the basics and think you know your tools, perhaps combining what you have already discovered with some of our ideas will give you new insights into their use and extend your technique.

The Work Area

It is easy for us to say that you don't need much room to paint on glass—which is true. But we have a large studio that we devote to stained glass, a portion of which is set aside for painting. Just how much is so devoted in actual measurements we cannot tell; when we paint we tend to use most of the surfaces and floor space around. We recognize that you may not have this kind of space, but you should have enough space to be comfortable—which includes standing back some distance to view and admire or criticize your work. Above all, don't make things so uncomfortable for yourself that your painting becomes a chore. It should be a pleasure, but if your surroundings are impossible, you will likely not experience much fun and creativity in your painting—and that's what it is all about.

Your basement or your living room are two possibilities for work areas. All we ask is that you give yourself enough room to breathe. This is a must for doing any work in stained glass. Too many individuals work in bleak, choked-up little spaces, inhaling soldering fumes and other noxious by-products. All paint has a warning label

30

as far as ingesting the stuff; it isn't necessary to breathe it in, either. Aside from that there is a question of comfort. You will be using vinegar, and perhaps as you go along certain oils and alcohols. Allowance should be made for enough air to dissipate these odors. One of the great pleasures of painting is ease. You can pick it up and put it down at your leisure. You should never let anything pressure you in this regard, certainly not your surroundings.

*Windows and
Overhead
Lighting*

Stained glass painting requires a specific light source that is transmitted through the glass working surface. The amount of reflection of other lighting from this working surface should be minimal. In fact, all reflected light should be subordinate to that coming from below or behind the glass. Too much reflective light, either from lights in the room or daylight through a window, can make it hard to see what you are doing. That doesn't mean you should be working in darkness except for your light table or easel light. But you should have some control over light reflecting off your work either by pulling a drape or a shade. Some painters even mask out portions of their light table that are not directly needed for the work at hand to take the strain off the eyes from all this upward pouring of light.

Figure 4-1 shows an ideal setting. Natural light comes through a window which is equipped with a shade so the light may be controlled by the worker. Below the window is the tracing table-easel. Behind the work surface is a curtain to keep extraneous lighting from penetrating the area. An artificial light behind the worker

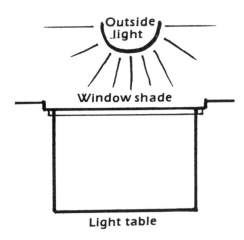

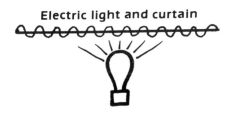

Fig. 4-1 Diagram of an
ideal lighting set-up.

may be utilized when necessary. Most painting areas have to compromise on certain of these elements; ideally it would be nice to have them all.

Anything you can do to focus the light through the work, without making the room so dim that you lose perspective, will help. It can take a bit of experimenting to get the lighting just right, but it is well worth the time and effort. Any area can be made comfortable and effective in this regard with a little ingenuity.

Water

A source of water should be available near your work area, but don't worry if you are working in your basement and the sink is a floor above. You will need water for your painting, but it needn't be running water—you can make do nicely with a cupful of water at a time, which should suffice for your painting. When you want to wash your brushes out at the end of your painting session, it is easy enough to carry them upstairs to the sink.

Incidentally, you may be concerned about the paints staining your sink. Even though the paints are water soluble, you may not like the idea of them going against your good enamel. The solution is to put your dirty water right down the drain or use the laundry tub. If you are using your kitchen sink to wash out brushes, etc., you should wash away all traces of paint before putting any food in the basin.

Storage

The more tools and supplies you have on hand, the more inconvenient it can be. This can make you less, not more effective.

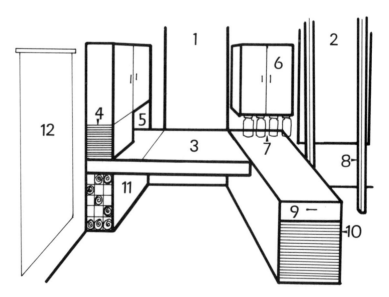

Fig. 4-2 An ideal studio for painting. (1 and 2) Windows; (3) Light table; (4) Palette box; (5 and 6) Storage; (7) Trace and matt paints; (8) Easel placement; (9) Brush storage; (10) Rack for cut, traced, and painted pieces; (11) Cartoon rack; (12) Cartoon mounting for viewing during painting on easel.

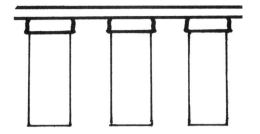

Fig. 4-3 One can store paint in small mounted jars which can be kept out of the way beneath a shelf.

Therefore, in planning out your work area, you should allow for storage niches and shelves. Figure 4-2 shows an ideal studio with plenty of storage space.

Use things at hand for storing your supplies. Baby food jars, for instance, are very good to store paint in. The paper packets that paint comes in are awkward to store. They develop holes, they get paint dust all over them, they are difficult to find, difficult to measure from. Baby food jars are good paint storers. You can make a hole in the center of the lid and attach the lid with a screw to the bottom of a shelf. The attached lid will now hold the jar in place (figure 4-3), and your paints will always be in front of your eye.

Brushes are best stored lying flat. Cigar boxes are good to keep them in, as is any small toolbox (figure 4-4). Many workers store their brushes upside down in a jar, but this is not recommended because it can give the bristles an unwanted flare.

Paint palettes are stored in a palette box (we tell you how to make one later in this chapter). Allow room for this box on your worktable. A very important storage area should be calculated for drawings and cartoons. These may be stored rolled up both to save room and for protection.

Fig. 4-4 A clutch of painting materials, stored flat in a tool box.

Clear glass squares for practicing painting can be stored in wire separators as used for records. Dish separators may be used if the partitions are deep enough.

You may not be able or want to get as elaborate as the storage units shown in our diagram. On the other hand, you may want to go beyond it. Use your imagination and your judgement. The point is to be comfortable and efficient. Remember that the most beautiful bins and shelves in the world won't help if you don't take the time to use them.

Temperature and Humidity

The area you choose to work in should not be too damp or too cold or too humid—not only for your own comfort, but also for the comfort of your paint. Vinegar trace paint seems especially susceptible to changes in humidity. We've had instances where an entire project, the work of several hours, was undone because of the vinegar trace paint going "bad" from the humidity—at least that was the only thing we could find to blame it on and it did seem better next day when the humidity was less.

It seems best to eliminate as many of the variables as possible from an activity that can be so disconcertingly imposed upon by the elements. Some sort of air conditioning in the summer, and perhaps a humidifier or dehumidifier in the winter can be all that is needed. If you are painting at home, chances are you are already equipped with these items. If you aren't, don't run out and immediately air condition your house just to improve the quality of your painting. You may not be having trouble in the first place. All we are suggesting is that if you find consistent problems cropping up and you believe you are doing everything just so, you may have to look elsewhere than your technique for their source.

Ventilation

You don't need a hood or a fan going when you paint; nor do you have to keep the windows open, but proper ventilation should be stressed when working with chemicals, and glass paint qualifies as such. As you advance with your painting technique, other chemicals will be involved. Get into good work habits now. If you abuse any craft process it will end up abusing you. We hate to have to stress this, as glass painting is probably the least health-threatening activity we know. Unfortunately people do tend to get careless if one doesn't insert certain cautions. So let us just make the point, and you take it from there.

Cleanliness and Dust

Keep your work area free of clutter. The fewer the miscellaneous items you have to stumble over, the more effective you will be in your craft.

The paint brushes, paints, spatulas, and glass palettes, to mention just a few of the items you will be using, all cost money. Their lives can be greatly prolonged by maintaining them in optimum condition. Brushes caked with last week's paint on their bristles, or carelessly put down in puddles of sticky gum or oil, or left in the sink where chemicals may be poured on them will hardly be able to do their best for you, and this will be apparent in the quality of work you turn out.

Careless handling not only cuts down on the quality of excellence built into your tools, but it can also result in a frustrating waste of time if you are hit with a sudden notion, go to express it in paint, and are not able to find just the item needed to transfer the idea from your mind onto the glass. It's awfully tempting, just to seize on some other item that happens to be handy to do the job. That's scarcely being fair to your own endeavor.

It's a lot easier to put your hand on the right brush or spatula if you don't have to scramble for it under a load of debris. Clutter is a nuisance and a drag on your creative energy in any craft; when you are working with pieces of glass it can be downright dangerous. Try to develop good working habits: as you finish with a particular item, put it away. Before you start any project, line up all your materials, have a place for each, and return each to its place when you have completed using it.

Be careful about food and drink around your workspace. Make certain your hands are clean before nibbling on that sandwich or piece of fruit. Glass paint on your hands is not a particularly welcome ingredient into your stomach; in fact there could be items in it that are injurious. Keep aware that you have food and drink around. If you don't, you'll find yourself dipping your paintbrush into your coffee with no consequent improvement in your painting technique. Needless to say, keep all paints away from children.

The area you work in needn't be dust-free—if there is such a thing. The normal amount of dust in the air won't influence your paint. At the same time, it would not be a good idea to overlook possible pollution problems in your immediate environment. If there is machinery nearby—for instance, a power saw sending great amounts of sawdust all over—it would behoove you to keep your painting far away from it. If you leave your paint overnight on your palette, you may find some dust has settled into it. Just blow it off the dried paint and you can reuse it with no problem. Some people advise covering your palette paint with plastic wrap or a watch glass to keep it clean. Remember, paint costs money. There is no reason to throw away the paint on your palette just because it may get or has gotten dusty.

Grease and grime in your paint, however, is another problem. If you have stored your palette in some area where it gets actually impregnated with such dirt, then, of course, you have no recourse but to dispose of it and mix a fresh batch. It needn't happen, however, if you exercise precaution in caring for your tools. The usual manner in which the glass painting student overspends money on supplies is through sheer waste or ignorance of needs. We don't want this to happen to you.

Clear Glass and Its Use

You will want to have plenty of clear glass on hand. You should be able to get scrap from your local glazer; as long as it isn't too small, you can use it. Cut it into squares or rectangles, clean it, removing all traces of putty, sand the edges, and take the corners down. You will be doing a lot of handling of these glass blanks and you don't want to cut yourself.

You will need at least two thicknesses of clear glass. The first is ordinary window glass, approximately ⅛ inch thick; the second is plate glass ¼ inch thick. The clear window glass is to practice your painting on so you don't waste your more expensive colored glasses learning the basics. The technique of painting on stained and clear glass is exactly the same. However, it is much cheaper to fire your mistakes onto clear glass than stained glass. Even if you are only practicing painting without firing, there is little use in cutting some of your good stained glass into squares to paint on. You have the additional advantage in practicing on clear glass in that you don't need a light table right away. You can place the sketch you will be tracing on a piece of white paper, put your window glass directly over it, and begin your tracing practice.

This doesn't mean you have to stick only to clear glass. As you go along, you will find it a good idea to get some very light tints of flesh-colored stained glass to try out the effect of your painting. Using flesh-colored glass will give a better idea of how the painting will "read." This is especially true when you get into the use of matt, the essential purpose of which is to modify and provide a value base for the already existing color in the glass. While trace paint will give pretty much the same effect on clear window glass as stained glass, matt paint is quite another thing entirely. However, for practicing the initial use of these paints, there is nothing quite so convenient and demonstrative as clear window glass.

The plate glass will be used for two purposes. The first is to make yourself some palettes; the second to use in your light table and easel. Let us look at these two items a little more closely.

Making Glass Palettes

As in oil painting, painting on glass requires palettes on which to mix and blend your colors. You will be mixing the paint with a number of materials, maybe even with other paints. However, unlike oil painting, you will use *one palette per color*. Each color of matt, trace, or stain should have its own palette. Of course, you can use just one palette if you wish, but this means washing off all remnants of the preceding color before mixing the next. This is a great waste of paint and time. We strongly advise using a different palette for each color, making yourself a palette box to store them in, and building up a repository of paints as you go along. Initially you should have at least the three palettes we have described above: for trace, for stain, and for matt.

Your palettes can be made out of either ¼-inch clear plate glass or a sandblasted piece. The sandblasted glass will cost a little more, but the surface furnishes the necessary resistance to help in mixing your color. The palette size can be anything you wish. We have found the most practical size to be approximately 14″ x 14″. Whether you buy a piece of sandlbasted glass or smooth plate glass, make sure that before you do anything with it you sand down the edges and round off the corners. This will prevent careless cuts as you concentrate on making it into a palette and during its use as one.

If you are going to make your own palette from a piece of smooth plate glass, all you need do is roughen the surface in the center. On a 14" x 14" piece of glass, this central roughened circle need only have a diameter of six or seven inches. The simplest way to do this is to grind some Carborundum (silicon carbide) grit into the glass. The procedure involves purchasing a glass muller, but since you will probably need this item as you go along, you might as well get it now. Mullers are available from many suppliers of glass paints and accessories. Mullers come in different sizes; you can easily determine what size best fits your purposes. Carborundum grit is available at your local hardware store. We got ours at Sears.

To roughen up your palette, place a few pinches of Carborundum and a small amount of water in the center of the glass and grind away with your muller (figure 4-6). Use a minimum circular motion and a reasonable amount of pressure. Your palette should be on an even surface, on a layer of newspaper. Keep checking to see the state of results as you go along (figure 4-7). The glass will become cloudy where it is being ground. If you hold it up to the light, you will see it becoming more and more translucent. Feel it with your finger to see how much rougher it is than the surrounding glass. The whole process shouldn't take you more than ten or fifteen minutes. The finished palette is shown in figure 4-8. When you mix your color on this palette, you will, of course, be mixing it over this ground area.

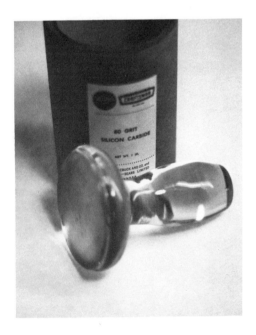

Fig. 4-5 The glass muller.

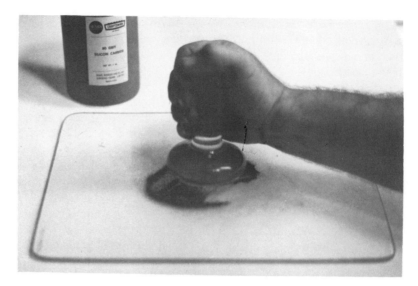

Fig. 4-6 Grinding Carborundum into the glass.

The Palette Box

Glass palettes are handled carelessly by many beginners who are more in a hurry to begin their painting than to build a supply depot. We can sympathize with this, but we must warn that if you don't take things in order you will sow the seeds of future confusion. Palettes should be stored in a palette box, not on shelves. Usually the palette is wider than the shelf, and it will tip off and break. Often the palettes simply end up one on top of another, contaminating the paint for future use. Occasional contamination can also occur from other items on the shelf or the shelf above.

A palette box is a closed container with runners on either side to

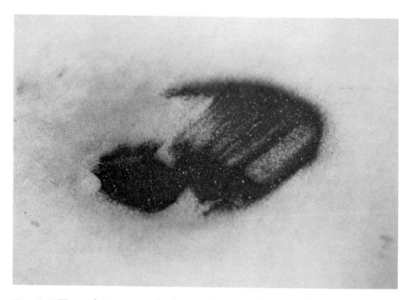

Fig. 4-7 The palette center begins to show roughening due to grinding.

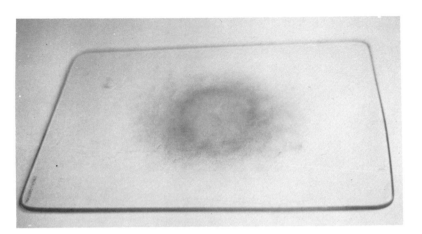

Fig. 4-8 Finished palette showing roughened center, sanded edges, and rounded corners.

Fig. 4-9 A standard palette box showing the runners and several palettes in place. This is quite a large box, designed for class-room use. Yours may be half this size, or less, de-pending on how much painting you will be doing.

fit your palettes (figure 4-9). It does not take long to build one. All your palettes should be made the same size so as to fit in the box. The size of the box is up to you. Make it large enough to accom-modate more palettes than you need initially, since you will be using more palettes as you progress in your painting technique.

Fig. 4-10 A palette box
made from two speaker
cabinets.

We use a palette box made from two small speaker cabinets put
together to achieve the requisite depth (figure 4-10). Our palette
box can accommodate eleven palettes. It is nineteen inches high,
twelve inches deep and eleven inches wide. Wooden strips support
the individual palettes inside. The side supporting the glass is $\frac{1}{2}$
inch wide; the one-inch thick side is against the side of the box to
furnish support for nailing.

Don't crowd your palettes together; leave enough room to get
your fingers in to reach out a palette. The pieces of glass should
slide in and out easily, yet be sufficiently supported so they won't
fall off their runners even if the box is carried from place to place.
We also advise you to put a backing on your palette box; that is,
don't leave it open at both sides. It can be convenient this way if
more than one person is painting and the palette box is placed between two work areas, but we have found in the long run such a
convenience is a false saving. The palette box will be much
stronger with a backing—it has an alarming tendency to tip to one
side or another without it. Furthermore, with a back on it the palettes will be placed evenly within the box rather than sticking out
one side or another in a jagged array that invites accidents.

On the side of your palette box you should label just what is on
the corresponding palette. Some people also put the date the paint
was mixed, although we don't feel that is necessary. The type of
color should also be labeled on the palette itself; the simplest way
to do this is to scrape it into the paint.

The Easel

Clear glass is also used for the easel. We will discuss here what
many studios use as a standard easel; when we discuss the light
table we will show you how you can combine easel and light table
together.

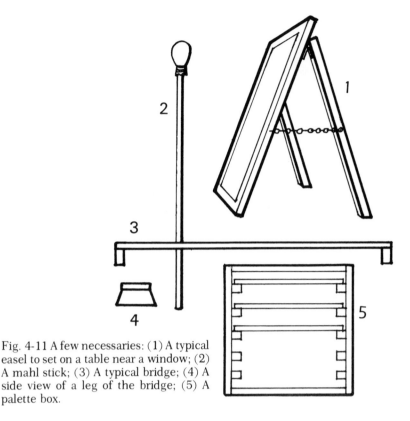

Fig. 4-11 A few necessaries: (1) A typical easel to set on a table near a window; (2) A mahl stick; (3) A typical bridge; (4) A side view of a leg of the bridge; (5) A palette box.

An easel for glass painting is a piece of glass raised upright on which stained glass pieces may be "waxed up" for ease in matting. Easels are made using plate glass 1/4 inch to 1/2 inch thick (if a great deal of glass is going to be waxed up). The reason for using plate glass this thick is to prevent the glass breaking under the weight of the glass and the pressure of the mahl stick on which you will be resting as you work.

To make a simple easel you can use two long angle irons (or steel shelving angles for a small easel) joined together top and bottom with supports (metal or heavy wood strips) for the clear glass. You must remember to secure your easel glass into the form with pegs or brackets so that it doesn't slide out and break. This easel may be leaned against a wall that has a window for a light source (natural light being always best for glass painting). The angle of the easel should be almost straight with the vertical, but naturally you don't want the angle too straight, or you will have the glass falling off the easel or the easel itself tipping forward. Wedge a box or wooden blocks under the tilted easel to support it as it leans against the wall.

If you are doing only small pieces of glass, a few at a time, and you have neither the space nor the inclination to make a large easel, you can make a table easel utilizing natural light (figure 4-11) or a self-supporting, self-lighting easel from a small light box held on a stand as seen in figure 4-12. Here we used the support from a child's blackboard into which we fixed an x-ray view box,

Fig. 4-12 Child's blackboard stand made into an easel. The light is furnished by a second-hand x-ray view box.

which are available, used, from surgical supply houses at quite
reasonable prices. We replaced the plastic surface with a piece of
ground glass, and it works perfectly well for individual painting endeavors. It is easy enough to move wherever you want it and the
angle can be almost vertical—a great help in getting your perspective correct.

The size of your easel depends on how large a piece of glass you
will be working on and how much of it will be painted. It's a good
idea to see all the glass that is going into a particular section,
whether it is all going to be painted or not, so you can study how
all the colors blend with the painting and with one another. Most
hobbyists, at least, will not be painting large church windows and
can limit the size of their easels to a piece of plate glass, maybe 3'
x 3'.

The Light Table

The light table is not the same as a light box, which is used
primarily to display stained glass. The light table is a working surface suffused with illumination. It is generally used for applying
graphic delineation; that is, tracing, stick-lighting, and diapering.

Light tables come in all sizes and shapes, and those who have already worked in stained glass are certainly familiar with the standard run of them. We are going to describe one with a certain modification, designed specifically for use with glass painting.

In a light table, the light comes from underneath and is spread over the surface as evenly as possible. Fluorescent lighting is most frequently used, because incandescent bulbs tend to create "hot spots," which will have you seeing spots before your eyes for some time after you leave the table, and because they are hot and dry the tracing color too quickly. The further down from the surface you can put your lights, the better the spread of light on the surface, the less clustering of light you will get from the individual fluorescent tubes. If your bulbs are strong enough you can just invert a fluorescent fixture resting on a couple of two by fours under the table. If you want to spread the light more evenly over a large surface, you can box in your light and cover the inside surfaces of the box with a reflective material such as aluminum foil.

Ground or diffusing glass should be used on the surface of the light table, though we have found a better and brighter light spread from a piece of white plastic lying under a plate glass top. The plastic diffuses the light to every corner of the table. Make certain the top of your light table is flat; that is, there should be no raised edges of moulding to interfere with the use of your bridge.

Our light table (figure 4-13) is a combination light table and easel. The top portion is hinged so that it can be swung up and braced for use during the matting process. This eliminates the need for a separate easel, and this type of easel can also be used with natural light. It is a very convenient spacesaver and timesaver

Fig. 4-13 Combination light table and easel. When down, it forms a light table (or part of one), and when up it's an easel. *Courtesy of American Glass Guild.*

Fig. 4-14 A large easel-light table for classroom use. *Courtesy of S.G.A.A.
School, Hoosuck, MA.*

because the same piece of glass can be traced, waxed, and matted
without having to move it to another piece of equipment. If you
wish, you can use smaller pieces of glass as the surface of your
light table, hinging them individually so you don't have to swing
up a heavy single piece of glass to matt a small amount of work.

Figures 4-14 and 4-15 show a lengthy light table used in teaching classes. The top is composed of multiple easels that can be
raised or lowered depending on what the student is working on at
any particular time. As seen in figure 4-14, the support stick is
anchored firmly into a slot in the rear board. When the easel lies
flat, this stick hangs free below the level of the table. The stick is
hinged to the top of the easel. Of course this is a specialized item,
but you may want to tailor the notion to your own needs.

The ideal spot for placement of a light table is in front of a window, provided you are able to mask out the light from the window
at will and use the light from the table alone. There are several ad-
vantages to having your table in such a spot. With a combination
easel/table, this allows you to use natural daylight to paint by,
always an advantage since you will get a much truer sense of color
than with artificial light. It also seems to be easier on the eyes if
you can adjust the amount of natural light around the table so
there is not an abrupt contrast between absolute darkness in the
room and the bright light from the table.

Some painters try to mask out all parts of the illuminated surface
they are not using to avoid excess light glaring up at them as well
as to enable focusing solely on the subject matter on hand. There

Fig. 4-15 Side view of the easel in figure 4-14. The support stick, hinged to the top of the easel, is anchored firmly into a slot in the rear board. *Courtesy of S.G.A.A. School, Hoosuck, MA.*

is a saying in the trade that glass painters' eyes go bad after a while from all the light they are constantly looking into. Perhaps if you do this sort of thing day after day for many years, your eyes may be affected, though we have never spoken to anyone who actually had this happen. It could be just another one of the mystiques of glass painting.

The mahl stick is a hand rest used for support when working on the easel. Since one end of it will be resting directly on the glass of the easel, it is necessary for it to be padded to avoid its either breaking the glass or slipping over its surface. The mahl stick is held at the unpadded end by the non-painting hand. If you are right-handed, you would hold the mahl stick in your left hand, across your body to the easel. Your right hand, doing the work, would dictate the position the mahl stick should be in. Sign painters and decorators use their mahl sticks to help make large sweeping strokes, almost compasslike in nature; they use it as a guide as much as a support. There is little motivation to use it in this manner in glass painting, in which it is used primarily as a support.

The Mahl Stick

You can easily make your own mahl stick from a ½-inch wooden dowel about 26 inches long. If it is much shorter than that, you will inhibit your arm motions; if it's much longer, it will become awkward. To pad the end of the mahl stick, several items can be used. We found the simplest to be a piece of thick kitchen sponge, cut dry in a circle about 1½ inches in diameter. Into the center of this we cut a hole the size of the dowel diameter and glued the sponge right to the end of the stick. The porous area of the sponge grabs the glass well and the amount of give at the end of the stick is just right.

A more standard method of making a mahl is to wrap one end of the stick with cotton and tie or tape a piece of rag over this (figure 4-16). Just tying a piece of rag, alone, over the end of the stick will not suffice because the stick will give too much point pressure against the glass. There should be between ½ to ¾ inch of soft material around the end of the stick.

We will have more to say about the use of the mahl stick and its cousin, the bridge, in succeeding chapters.

The Bridge

Like the mahl stick, the bridge is an item you can readily make yourself. Unlike the mahl stick, the bridge is not used solely for support; it is an integral part of your painting technique and you should spend some time on its construction.

The bridge is essentially three pieces of wood nailed together as shown in figure 4-11. We prefer a bridge that gives plenty of room for the arm to move along its length, yet not one that is so long it proves difficult to move it about. A lot depends on the size of your work table; the bridge shouldn't be so long that its end keeps going

Fig. 4-16 Mahl sticks on a light table. Note the padded end of each, stuffed with rag with the ends taped neatly around the stick.

off the edge. Generally we use a bridge between 20 and 22 inches in length and about 1½ to 2½ inches high. It's a good idea to put a few pieces of wood together to get a feel for what height and length you think will serve you best, keeping in mind that you may experience a certain awkwardness under the best of circumstances if you've never used such an item before.

Your bridge is a very personal tool. Some people like to have very stiff wood along the span so their hand is completely sturdy; other prefer a little resiliency. Either way, there should certainly be no wobbling of the bridge, and so it is a good idea to glue all the supports together before nailing them. Naturally, both end pieces must be cut exactly even and their surfaces be flush with the table. As long as you are making one bridge, you might as well make a couple. It helps to have a spare for those occasions when you are in a hurry to get going and have misplaced your bridge.

Once you have your bridge together, sand it. The top surface along which your arm is going to move should be very smooth so a free-flowing motion can be obtained. Also, of course, you don't want any splinters. All nails should be flush with the surface so you don't catch yourself on any ragged edges.

For purposes of demonstration, our own bridge is 1¼ inches wide across the span, ⅜ inches thick and 2¼ inches high. The span overlaps both end supports, which gives additional strength to the span all along its length, though this is not essential; the end supports can be flush.

The Muller

We have mentioned the muller earlier in describing how you can make your own glass palette. A muller (see figure 4-5) is a grinder similar to a pestle. It is made of glass, not porcelain, and has a stem attached to a flat grinding surface, sort of like an upside-down mushroom. Aside from its use in making a palette, mullers are used to grind all gritty paints. Most of these are Hancock paints that require such treatment, though some workers grind all their paints with a muller when they first mix them, either out of habit, or just to take no chances. If you do not intend to make your own glass palettes, and if you are going to initially limit your color to Drakenfeld paints, you can probably do without buying a muller at this time. You can always buy one when you need it.

Gum Arabic

Gum arabic, often referred to simply as "gum," is an essential ingredient to most painting. It comes in both powder and liquid form (figure 4-17), and is available at most art supply stores. We have worked with both and have decided there is really no difference between the two so far as painted effect is concerned. There are a number of reasons for using this material which we will get to in a succeeding chapter. When you buy it, try to purchase a minimal amount. You will only be using a tiny bit of it at a time.

Fig. 4-17 Gum arabic—liquid and powder.

Palette Knives   It's a good idea to have a few palette knives on hand—one for trace, one for matt, one for stain, one for oil—so you don't have to keep washing off your only knife every time you want to mix something up. However, one will do if necessary. Palette knives (see figure 4-18), of course, are used to mix the color over the glass palette, to get the right consistency, and to make certain that all ingredients are properly blended. Rarely will you need the giant up top. Most commonly used are the two center examples and the left, thin blade which we use for mixing stain. For a mix that has heavy, gritty particles of paint, you might like the one on the ex-

Fig. 4-18 A selection of palette knives.

treme right. This can be used for a rough mix; then switch to one of the more flexible knives to achieve a smooth consistency.

The technique of mixing paint with these particular spatulas will be gone into in another chapter. All palette knives should be cleaned of paint at the end of each session; don't leave them on the palette to cake into the unused paint. Because these knives are constantly being honed through their use, they can develop edges as sharp as any true knife. Don't run your finger over the edge of your palette knife to see how sharp it is; take our word for it. Every so often you should use a piece of Carborundum paper along the sides of these knives to round off their edges.

Wax

We use two types of wax: beeswax and "thumb" wax, a recipe for which is given below. The beeswax can be used by itself or mixed with resin to make it stiffer. It is used to hold the pieces of glass to the easel during the waxing up process. You can purchase resin and chunks of beeswax at your paint supplier. It is heated in a pot (one that you do not intend to use for anything else) over a burner. You do not have to use a double boiler to heat the beeswax—it is an unnecessary inconvenience. It heats up more quickly, of course, and routine precautions should be observed to make sure you don't burn yourself and that the wax doesn't catch fire. Should it do so have a cover ready to place on the pot (we've never had any problem with this). Glass medicine droppers are great for transferring the melted beeswax to the corners of the glass that is to be stuck up on the easel. We like to drill a hole in the pot handle as a handy place to keep our medicine dropper. One can never seem to find it, otherwise.

Under no circumstances should the melted beeswax be allowed to run down the surface of the glass. If the beeswax is too soft, add more resin. The glass is removed from the easel by putting a spatula or small "chipping" knife under a corner; the beeswax should chip away from the pressure if you have the right amount of resin in it.

Don't waste your used wax—simply throw it back into the pot. Don't worry if it has some paint in it—it works just as well clean or dirty. Most glass painters feel that wax isn't really any good until it has become mixed with a lot of color anyway and develops a professional "used" look.

Don't be fooled by a lot of recipes purporting to give a wax that will do a better job. The additions of all sorts of weird substances have been proposed, each purporting to at last reveal the true secret of some sort of magic wax. There is no secret to wax. Many studios use pure beeswax, period, without even adding resin, though we advise that you add this substance to make removing the glass from the easel an easier task. Too much resin in a cold atmosphere and you'll have your glass falling off the easel just from the vibration of someone walking across the room. In this, as in so much else in painting, you must do some experimenting for yourself. As a rule of thumb, the proportions of wax and resin vary according to the season. In the winter you generally use less resin; in the summer a good bit more. Wax is the malleable portion of the mixture; the resin the more resistant ingredient.

Thumb wax, which has the consistency of firm putty, is not meant to get hard. It is usually held in a ball in one hand and pieces of it are pinched off as needed by the other hand. It is used for quick, temporary stick-ups on the easel, either for pieces of glass or pattern. For example, glass painters may stick samples of glass onto the easel when changing a color or type of glass; some workers place the pattern on the easel, held with thumb wax, for color selection. It is, of course, much more convenient to use thumb wax than beeswax for such purposes. Placing glass on the easel in this manner is called "stopping in." You can put a number of pieces of glass on the easel with thumb wax, take them down and substitute others. Once you've decided the proper glass replacement, these can be "locked in" with the beeswax.

Here is one formula for thumb wax, courtesy of Jack Cushen from Robert Metcalf:

1 pound beeswax (453 grams)
1 pound cornstarch (453 grams)
4 ounces resin (113 grams)
7 ounces Venice Turpentine (198 grams)
1 3/4 ounces "sweet oil" (olive oil- measure 35 cc)

Melt the wax in a double boiler. Add cornstarch a tablespoon at a time, stirring the mixture thoroughly after each spoonful. Then add the resin, turpentine, and oil. When thoroughly mixed, pour into a muffin or cookie tin and allow to cool.

Needles, Quills, Penpoints, Sticks

Quills, needles, penpoints, and sticks (figure 4-19) are all used for "taking out the lights," stick-lighting or highlighting of one form or another. Each of these items is utilized to produce a certain effect. None of them should be used as a crutch to correct limitations in dexterity, to clean up shoddy trace lines, for instance. These items are extremely useful for diapering, stick-light outlining, highlighting hairlines, for sharply removing points and exposing light. We will show you how they are used in these particular techniques as they come up.

You should provide yourself with good tools. Needles are easily come by. Penpoints can be purchased. Use them in an old penholder—you will be more dexterous with it this way than with the point in your hand. As for quills, these are wonderful for fine outlining as in hair. You can use a quill from a duck, and a goose quill is excellent. Many towns have live poultry stores (check your yellow pages). It is worth going to some trouble to acquire a supply of quills. You will have to resupply yourself occasionally as they tend to dry out in time, but they make wonderful instruments for certain purposes.

The sticks you use should be made from one of the hardwoods. We like to make one end of the stick pointed, the other end chisel-shaped. The stick is very important in diapering, especially, and if

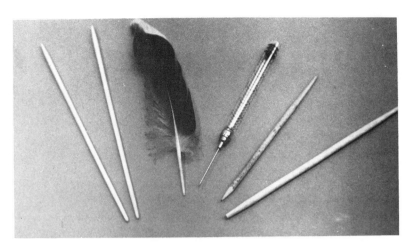

Fig. 4-19 Needles, quill, penpoints, and sticks. The needle need not be so
ornate, but it is best to have a handle on it.

it is a softwood stick, it will begin blunting at the point and edges
and develop burrs that will catch and chip the paint instead of
cleaving it. You can purchase suitable sticks, or make you own
from any narrow hardwood dowel.

We have also found in the past that chopsticks offered in Orien-
tal restaurants are excellent for making the sticks. We say "in the
past" because it seems that many of these restaurants are now
using chopsticks of quite inferior material. The good chopsticks
are made from bamboo, a very delightful hardwood. What the new
ones are made from we don't know—pressed fortune cookies, perhaps. Ask your waiter for the good chopsticks—he'll know what
you mean—and tell him you want to take them home. Also, many
kitchenware departments and stores have them for sale, as do ori-
ental specialty shops.

While we are on the subject, don't use hard metal pointed ob-
jects instead of wood for stick-lighting. The metal tends to slide on
the glass and will perhaps ruin your work.

❧ CHAPTER 5

Brushes: Technique and Pitfalls

Brushes have different shapes and they are made from different materials. This can be rather confusing. Confronted by a variety of brushes in a supplier's catalog, all different in configuration as well as in type of hair, all bearing strange names, the novice is tempted to throw up his hands in dismay, What is the suitability of each, and which one to purchase?

We will recommend certain brushes to start with. You choice is not limited to these, however, but we have always found it a good idea, when learning, to make haste slowly. Buy what you need, a little at a time. Learn to use each item well before incorporating new tools and techniques in your repertoire—you'll find the new tools and techniques come easier that way.

The brushes described below are all you will need to begin your painting study. Most people are astonished at this, pointing to the great variety of brushes described in the Reusche catalog, brushes dealing with techniques from scrolling to shading, from grounding to tinting. But these brushes are meant for china painting and have little or nothing to do with painting on glass. Even the names of such brushes—riggers, banders, grounders—apply directly to china painting. (Certain special brushes in the Reusche catalog do apply to glass. Such brushes as deerfoot stipplers, certain of the tinting brushes, and other specialty brushes are used for the oil and alcohol techniques of glass painting—a subject beyond the scope of this book.)

If you want to experiment with any of the china painting brushes as you go along, you are certainly free to do so, but chances are you you will be duplicating an effect easily derived from one of the glass painting brushes we describe. In fact you will be quite pleased to discover the number of effects you can produce just from the tracer and badger alone. We suggest that initially you will have plenty to do getting used to the essential brushes directly applicable to glass. All sorts of other possibilities for texturing exist, such as newspaper, sponges, toothbrushes, or what have you. But the brushes described below are all you will have to buy—and these purchases will last you for a long, long time.

52

Silver stain has been applied as a wash, and now the excess is being removed with a highlight brush prior to firing. Note the brown color of the unfired stain. Once it is wiped off after firing, the golden color will appear.

A head, showing how random application of stain can give a free-flowing effect to the hair.

The vine after firing. The Hebrew lettering is an example of the power of positive inscribing even on plain "white" glass.

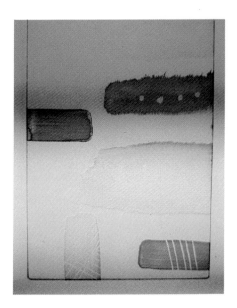

Test firings of various dilutions of stain for depth of color, blending ability, and adherence to the glass.

Examples of negative inscribing and diapering on various colors of stained glass. *Richard Millard*.

Lion head. A dramatic presentation utilizing trace, matt, and etching. *Richard Millard*.

Fragment of border, with matt, trace, and silver stain. A lot of design on one small area of glass, but done so tastefully that nothing looks crowded and no single element overpowers another. A nice study in effective artistry.

Hand painted with Rouge Jean Cousine.

Miniature head painted as the central focus within a decorative panel. *Courtesy of C. P. Mercadante.*

Fragment (releaded), showing effect of trace and silver stain against white glass. Note how the background is blacked out. *Courtesy of Richard Millard.*

Unicorn, painted by Andrew Daugherty from a design by Alice V. Scott (©). Black trace and faint highlighting over thin wash of matt. *Courtesy of Andrew Daugherty and Alice V. Scott.*

Baseball player, demonstrating trace, silver stain, and matt. *Courtesy of Gaytee Studios.*

Window design utilizing graphic painted detailing. *Anita Isenberg.*

Fish rondel window, with trace, matt, and etching on colored glass. *Richard Millard.*

Textured and stained glass, augmented by paint and enamel (flesh tones). *Courtesy of Gaytee Studios.*

Section of a large window, showing trace, matt, and stain.

We have found it a good idea, even when beginning your glass painting, not to stick to just one brush for a specific technique. No matter how comfortable it gets to feel in your hand, experiment with others, other sizes of tracers, riggers, and so forth, so that your hand develops a stroke that will compensate for different brushes. Each brush will give you a different result, not necessarily better in all instances, but you will find your efficiency increased by knowing which brush will best do the job you have in mind. The more brushes you get used to, the more adept you will become, the more expansive your capacity. That doesn't mean you have to buy every brush in the catalog, but you should start out with three or four of the ones we will be describing.

Brushes usually come with some sort of protection for their bristles—either a cardboard or a plastic sleeve. It isn't necessary to use these if you keep your brushes properly. Laying them flat is best. Keeping them handle down in a glass is probably worst as the bristles will tend to flair outwards. Some people like their blender bristles with this outward flair and purposely keep them upside down. There is a handy little device (figure 5-1) to hang wet brushes in to dry so their hairs will not be deformed by touching anything. We recommend that you get one of these if you are going to do any substantial amount of work with various brushes. It is awkward, to say the least, to reach for a tracer you've used a

Fig. 5-1 Brush holder.

short time ago and find the hairs curled up into a C shape due to the way you left it. With reasonable care, not only will your brushes last a long time, they will always be ready for use.

When you go to use a brand new tracing brush, you will probably find the bristles quite stiff. The hairs of many of these brushes are coated with some protective ingredient, usually gum arabic. It is a good idea to dip any brand new brush in water before using it for painting. Give it a good soaking and let the bristles splay out.

It may take a little while to get used to the character of a new brush. You may have to do some fiddling with it, turning it in your hand and trying it from every angle to get its proper feel. Because of the manner in which the brush hairs are placed in the ferrule, the brush may appear to have a top and bottom to the bristles when wet. That is to say the "bottom" may appear slightly rounder; the top somewhat flat. No matter how you turn the brush, it will attempt to re-establish itself in this fasion. Many painters deny that this is the case, but we feel each brush is an individual and you may run into one that has this peculiar "set." If so, paint with the flatter side up, rounded down. It is a very subtle characteristic, but if you think your brush has it, try using it in this way.

The Badger Blender

Badger hair is used to make one of the most important of all glass painting brushes, the badger blender (figure 5-2). This brush is used in the matting process and is the most expensive brush you will be buying. The badger blender costs rather a lot, but for the effects it produces, it is worth it. It is used to distribute the applied matt paint over the glass surface, to gather the matt into specific areas, and to blend all these areas together. You may want your matt spread uniformly or irregularly, thick or thin, patterned or bland, smooth or cross-hatched. This brush will do the job.

A typical badger blender is about eleven inches from tip of handle to end of bristle and four inches wide. However, they come in several sizes and shapes. They also come in at least two price ranges. We suggest that you do not mince pennies here, but get the more expensive. Buy the best available—you will end up saving money in the long run and will have an indispensable ally throughout your glass painting career.

Other brushes have been substituted for the badger, most popular among these being old-fashioned shaving brushes. While they may be worthwhile for individual effects (what brush isn't?), they do not have the dependability and sweep of the badger for even blending. Not over larger areas, in any event. No round brush can compete since the bristles tend to splay and flick the matt rather than take it across a wide, homogeneous plane.

If you are going to do any serious painting, a good badger blender should be among your first purchases. You get what you pay for. The cheaper blenders have thinner tufts of hair and are generally skimpier. Many of the cheaper blenders also tend to shed hair more readily as they are worked, and it is annoying when

Fig. 5-2 Two badger blenders: a less expensive one on the right, an expensive one on the left. Between them is the matting brush we like to use for matt application.

these hairs get into the matt as you are working it. You have to keep your eyes constantly open for these intruders, pick them out immediately while the matt is wet, and reblend the matt at that area. Often you will not notice these hairs until the matt has dried. In that case, after picking out the hair, you will probably have to reblend the entire scene. You will probably be ready to tear out your own hair at this point. It's worth it to get a good brush right from the beginning.

Round blenders are available as well as flat ones. We feel the same way about round blenders, however, as we do about the shaving brushes. The hairs may be stiffer, but the shape of the blender still mitigates against its most efficient use in a blending "sweep." All in all, we have not come up against a brush to replace the standard badger for peak efficiency. You'll be surprised how good a badger that knows its business can make you look.

It is important to keep the badger clean, and to clean it constantly while using it. Actually, only the tips of the hairs get wet, so cleaning the blender is not a big job—but it is a constant one. If any of the paint dries on the tips of the hairs, it will ruin the blending effect of the brush. The hairs will then tend to chip into the matt rather than spread it evenly. Excessive moisture on the hairs of the brush will also spoil the blending effect.

There are a couple of quick ways to clean off the blender. You can twirl it *bristles down* (so the material that comes flying off doesn't get into your hair and face); you can dust it against a stiff surface such as the corner of a cardboard box or a handy two-by-four or table leg; or you can dust it against your own leg if you don't mind a bit of paint there. Twirling it bristles down will spread the hair to the sides. Some workers prefer their blender in that shape, but if you do not, store it in the cardboard form. If you are going to dust your blender against something, please make sure it does not have sharp edges which can damage or snag the blender hairs—after all, you've paid good money for it.

If you can afford it, we suggest you purchase two blenders: an expensive one *and* a cheap one. Use the cheap one for stain. Silver nitrate stain tends to dry out the hairs of brushes and the blender is no exception. You can make the one expensive blender serve for all purposes, especially at the beginning, by keeping it immaculately clean when using it for stain, but as you go along, you may find it a saving in the long run to protect this original investment by getting hold of a cheap blender for staining purposes.

Tracers

The other basic glass painting brush is the tracer. Tracers are long-haired brushes that come to a point (figure 5-3). Their use is obvious from their name—they are meant to produce specific lines on the glass following an underlying pattern. Although they come in various sizes and are made from various types of hairs, their basic shape is always the same.

It has been our experience that the finest tracing brushes for basic painting techniques, and the ones that will best serve the purposes described in this book, are the Superior French Oxhair series 30, sizes 3, 7, and 9. The Camel Hair Tracer series 3 are excellent as well, although they tend to be very responsive to subtle variations of pressure, which can be disconcerting if you haven't done all that much tracing with them. This is due more to the configuration of the brush than the substance of the hair.

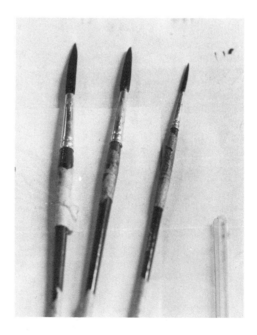

Fig. 5-3 Three tracing brushes, thick, medium, and thin. The plastic sleeve used to protect the sensitive bristles is in the lower right. Tracers can be wrapped with different colored tape to distinguish the particular vehicle they are used for.

The red sable brush is also a fine tool, though we consider it better suited to oil tracing, a technique not covered in this book. Red sable hair seems to be less porous than either oxhair or camel hair. It therefore does not seem to be able to hold as much paint as these other two brushes in the same controlled, adherent manner. A camel or oxhair brush will provide a more flowing, longer line in a single stroke. But a sable tracer is excellent for producing thin lines of paint in equal consistency throughout their length, whether using water or vinegar as the vehicle. In short, you can use a sable hair brush for very fine line detail; a camel or oxhair for a more flowing stroke with thick and thin variations. This does not mean there is not a great deal of crossover between the two. If we were going to get only one, we would get the oxhair. The best thing for the beginner, as we see it, would be to purchase the brush that is the most versatile: this would be an oxhair.

Incidentally, the camel brush is not made from camel hair. Camel is the name of the man who discovered the use of this particular brush; the hair itself comes from a Russian squirrel. Both camel brushes and red sable brushes, as well as all the brushes specific to glass painting and china painting, are handmade. They are put together by craftsmen expert in picking out just the right amount of compatible hair and binding it into the ferrule of the brush.

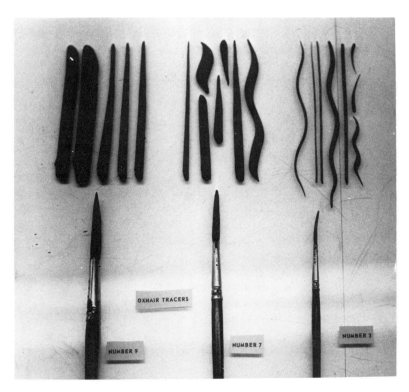

Fig. 5-4 Sizes 9, 7, and 3 oxhair tracers. Note how each size brush paints a totally different line, in width and in character.

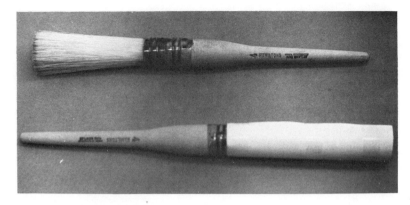

Fig. 5-5 Pig bristle stippler.

Size of tracers is another important consideration. Whatever hair you buy, we recommend you purchase three different sizes to begin with—a small, a medium, and a large (or thin, medium, and thick) from series 30 in the Reusche catalog (figure 5-4). This will enable you to get the feel of the difference in the brushes and what can be accomplished with them. We have found the most important sizes to be 3, 7, and 9. You can do most, if not all, your tracing with these sizes.

The idea of using a tracer is to get as much of a continuous flow of paint along the line with a single stroke as possible. That's why tracers have such long hairs in proportion to their width. A tracing brush, unlike a watercolor brush, is not meant to dab with. The idea is to keep the brush down, keep it moving, keep it steady, and outline whatever you are tracing with bold strokes. We will be discussing the technique of using these brushes later. It takes a little practice, but once you get it down, you will never forget how to use a tracer.

Stipplers

Stippling is a form of shading in which a myriad of tiny dots is formed in or with the matt. The matt can be laid on with a stippling brush to begin with, or the matt is applied with a blender and then stippled, or the dried matt is stippled with the bristles of the brush. Sometimes the blender hairs themselves are used to stipple with; often a pig bristle or other bristle brush is employed to provide the proper texture.

Pig bristle stipplers (figure 5-5) are formidable brushes, and at least one should be part of your brush collection. This brush has an interesting history. From 1950 to 1972 it was not available in this country since the pig bristles come from China. Apparently, only in that country, where pigs are kept as pets, do these animals live long enough to develop the hair length necessary to form the proper size for good stipplers.

A good stippling brush is next in importance to your tracers and your blender, and we recommend the English glass stainer's stippler series 32-A in the Reusche catalog. This brush provides a very sharp, distinct stipple which gives a very nice effect of depth from a distance. A good stippler will pay for itself many times over in the effects it will produce.

Bristle brushes are also used to make so-called scrubs or highlight brushes. These must undergo modification, and we will be discussing them in the chapter on highlighting. Bristle hair takes shaping well. One good thing about bristle brushes is that you can buy very cheap ones to be trimmed as highlight brushes, and if you have a friend who is a painter, ask to be given any bristle brushes he or she intends to throw out. They can't be used any longer for oil or watercolor painting, but for your purposes they can be just right.

Highlight Brushes

Correct application of the matt is as important as correct blending. Many students do not appreciate this fact and make their blending more difficult by applying the matt awkwardly to begin with. We like to apply matt in a very specific way and accordingly recommend a couple of specific brushes to do it with. For applying matt to the entire piece of glass we recommend the 1½ inch camel brush, series 18 in the Reusche catalog (see figure 5-6). This tends to lay on a very even coat of matt in a rapid manner, and with proper care it will last you a long time. (You can also use this brush as a small blender.) For pinpoint matting, as in applying shadow under eyes or alongside the nose or cheek, the ³/₈ inch or ½ inch tinting brushes will do this job very nicely. The blending of small shadows can be done with the badger or with another dry tinting brush.

Matting Brushes

Tinting brushes are generally used in ceramic rather than glass painting. They are fluffy, wide brushes, smaller though than the badger blender. They can be very useful in matting and blending

Optional Brushes

Fig. 5-6 Painting brushes. Clockwise from left: matting brush, tinting brush, deerfoot stippler, hard stippler.

discrete areas because their smaller size gives you more control and you can push the matt firmly into smaller spots. We often use a ¹/₂ inch Reusche series 16 tinting brush. You will not need tinting brushes right off, but will probably want to purchase some in the future.

A lettering brush is another optional brush, but if you intend to do any great amount of lettering, you should get one. Lettering is, after all, a tracing procedure when done from a cartoon. (See chapter 14, Inscriptions.) A lettering brush is usually a sable brush. It is usually cut chisel-straight across the end. This allows the square-shaped commencement and termination of a stroke that is particularly useful in the lettering process. The hair setting is parallel to enable an even consistency of width. Such brushes are available in most art supply stores in a variety of widths from ¹/₁₆ inches to 1¹/₂ inches. The wider brushes, which have a flat rather than round ferrule, also make very appropriate matting brushes.

A Chinese writing brush is another possibility. We do not recommend using a Chinese writing brush for the normal types of lettering generally done in windows. Its use requires an entirely different discipline than that employed with standard brushes. Pressure is everything here. With the Chinese lettering brush, too much variation in pressure results in either a sudden blob of paint or a skipped stroke. But it is a beautiful brush to play with, and it is one you might purchase in the future.

Basic Brush Technique

Teaching is a matter of repetition and we will be treating much of the following information in greater depth as we get into the actual work of painting. However, there are some generalities you should be introduced to as soon as possible as far as handling your brushes is concerned. Whatever brush you are using should be gripped firmly but gently. Don't hang onto it so that it begins to shake. The brush should become a natural extension of your hand. Hold a tracer, for instance, as you would hold a pencil. You want to utilize the full capacity of your brushes. You will learn to do this through appropriate motions of your fingers, wrist, and arm—and through *practice*.

A brief description of how each brush is used follows. Each technique is dealt with in depth in later chapters.

THE BADGER BLENDER

Contrary to the preconceived notion many students have, the blender is not a dusting brush. It is held delicately and just stroked over the glass *only* after it has first been used as a pusher to get the wet matt distributed where you want it. Use of the blender, then, is twofold: (1) to distribute the paint, and (2) to make it uniform over the surface.

Blending, which is discussed in detail in chapter 12, is done in a figure-8 pattern, each series of strokes going at right angles to the preceding one, making the cross lines so formed finer and finer until they disappear altogether. Don't get so involved with getting your strokes down that you keep hitting your blender against the sharp edge of the glass, because you will start cutting hairs. Bring your blender onto the glass surface like an airplane landing. Only the tips of the badger hairs touch the work, of course, but this is more than enough to spread the matt in the final smooth blending. Practice will show you how much pressure to apply to get just the tips of the hairs involved and no more.

THE TRACER

Tracers are built to hold a quantity of paint; the idea is to use everything the tracer has to offer. By varying the pressure of your hand, you will be able to get thick and thin areas within the line as you travel along. Each tracing stroke will be made as completely as possible before you change to the next stroke. This imparts the necessary flow to your line without your constantly having to pick up the brush and reapply it to the glass. This doesn't mean you cannot use two strokes where one is going to be obviously awkward. In such a case you will have to lift your brush, change position, and take up where you left off. But this shouldn't happen more than is absolutely necessary.

In making an initial tracing stroke that starts with a point, the brush should come firmly on the glass like an airplane landing. Don't tickle the surface irresolutely. As the brush hits the glass it should be completing an arc it has started some inches above. This doesn't mean you should slap the hairs against the glass so hard that paint spatters. If you begin your stroke just prior to coming in contact with the glass, you will get a much surer line and a more substantial carry-through to the end.

Good tracing is a matter of practice. You will be going over and

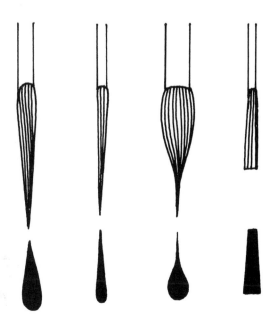

Fig. 5-7 Four tracing brushes showing the basic shape of different strokes. These strokes are the same whether the brush is oxhair, camel, or sable.

over the same strokes until your hand develops that spatial and physical relationship to the work which is the basic secret of good technique. Once you have the technique, you can trace anything you wish. For now, stay with us. We have developed certain exercises which will give your fingers, wrist, and arm a "tracing sense." You will be getting these in chapter 8. By the time you are done with them, use of the tracer will be second nature.

Cleaning your brush after using it is also basic brush technique. You should wash it well in lukewarm, not hot, water (a good rule for most brushes) and remember to work out the paint that may be clogging the back portion of the brush under the ferrule. (This is especially true for staining brushes where the stain may begin to eat through a metal ferrule if not washed away.)

All of us tend to get careless, and if you find you have left your tracer in the paint overnight and the bristles are splayed and stiff, or you've left it pressing against something and the bristles are curled into fetal position, don't discard the brush. It can be readily salvaged. All you have to do is clean the hairs with water and, while they are wet, use your fingers to mold them back into shape. You may also use a mild soap. Then put the brush in the refrigerator overnight. What you are doing is giving the brush a hair set. The bristles will go right back to the way they were when you bought the brush. As we have said, our own favorite tracers are the French oxhair brushes, series 30, in the Reusche catalog. Give them a hand and they'll do the work.

THE STIPPLER

There are two major ways of distributing and texturing the matt: the first is to badger it, the second to stipple it. Although the badger blender can be used as a stippler, we suggest you purchase a specific brush for this purpose because stippling is a very important method of treating the matt.

There are three types of stippling technique: wet, applied, and dry. One wet method is as follows. Matt is put on the glass with the matting brush just as if you were going to badger it. But instead you reach for your stippler and commence stabbing at the matt during the course of the matt's drying. You can achieve a myriad textures in the matt in this manner. You do not have to continue the process until the matt is dry; you can leave off at any time. You will get different effects depending on how long you continue the procedure. If the matt is still fairly wet when you stop, the final stipple will have a slightly blurry outline due to the still wet matt spreading somewhat back into the stippled areas. You can, of course, go right on merrily stippling throughout the time the matt is drying until all the water has evaporated. Depending, again, on when you leave off, you can develop an effect of very discrete dots in the surface as though the glass had been peppered. If you continue even beyond this point, you will start removing areas of matt so that you will have almost clear glass with very fine hazes of matt.

Fig. 5-8 (Upper left) Stippling, wet method. First the matt is laid down on the glass and blended.

Fig. 5-9 (Upper right) Using the badger blender as a stippler gives a very fine, grainy effect.

Fig. 5-10 (Left) Too much stippling seems monotonous? One swipe of the blender gives a swirling effect to interfere with the stipple.

Fig. 5-11 (Bottom left) Working the blender with the wrist in a small circular motion . . .

Fig. 5-12 (Bottom right) . . . results in an effect similar to this. Any of the three texturing effects noted here can be further modified, either with the blender or any other brush. Obviously texturing is not done for itself alone, as shown here, but to bring out some character or value of the glass or a particular element of painted detail.

An applied method of stippling is the application of matt with the stippler itself. One achieves areas of desired shading by placing specks of matt directly with the bristles rather than by picking out specks from a solid surface of matt.

Dry stippling is the removal of dried matt with a bristle stippler. You can use anything from a pig bristle stippler to those of bullet shape and others. One of the finest is the $3/16$ inch brush for truly concentrated highlights. The pig bristle stippler works beautifully for accomplishing subtle transitions from highlights to shadow. It produces a gradual, halation-like transposition from a central concentration of light to an encircling shadow since the outer hairs splay outward, thereby imposing less pressure on the glass.

There is, as you may imagine, a wide range of shading and texturing literally at your fingertips with a good stippler. A poor stippler will not give you the multiple tiny holes you want, but will just remove chunks of the matt in an irregular sort of way. You may want this effect sooner or later, and you should always be on the lookout for an old brush or two that will give you different stipple effects. However, to start with you should not depend on accident but use a good, standard stippler.

Stippling, a technique which dates from the fourteenth century, textures and shades the glass, but in a unique way. The fourteenth-century painters, absorbed in using heavy shadowing, found that through stippling they could get a deep effect of shadow and yet still allow light to come through—a process which created and enhanced the shadowing technique itself. The reason for this is due to the pinholes created by poking these bristles at the matt. You can barely see them as pinholes from any distance, but what you will see is a transmission of light through the shadow. As the light comes through these holes it seems to spread and radiate over the surface of the shadowed area. It illuminates the shadow, making it even more effective.

THE MATTING BRUSH

Placing the matt on the glass is not a matter of splashing it about haphazardly. You want it put on as efficiently and as evenly as possible. The strokes should cover the width of the glass and they should all run in the same direction for convenience. Don't use your badger blender to apply matt to the glass.

You may notice after the brush has become fairly soaked in matt that the hairs are liable to bend over to one side and remain in that awkward curl. Just dip the brush in water or turn it around and it will straighten out and you can go right back to using it.

Applying matt is not meant to be an artistic process, nor are we attempting to make it one. It should, however, be a neat and planned process that will allow you to accomplish your blending or stippling more efficiently. We will be discussing this further in the chapter on matting.

CHAPTER 6

Kilns and Firing

Since all applications of color described in this book require firing to bond the paint to the glass, in this chapter we would like to discuss a few of the details regarding kiln work. First of all, a kiln for painted glass work need not be expensive. Since you are going to be dealing with flat pieces, not three-dimensional ceramic greenware, a small kiln will do. Buy one with a pyrometer, which registers the temperature of the kiln as it fires. You can acquire a moderate size enameling kiln quite reasonably and, since you will not be heating nearly so high as you would for ceramic work, your electric bill will not suffer. Such a kiln, with room for two or three shelves, will do quite nicely if you are only painting occasional pieces. Of course, the more painting you do, the larger the kiln you will need—but you should realize that there is a great measure of adaptability here. Many individuals don't get into glass painting because they feel the expense of a kiln would be overwhelming. In fact, it is far from that, and when you consider the pleasure you will get out of it, it is cheap at the price whatever it may be.

Frequently the kiln shelves are prepared before firing with a coating of kiln wash that prevents the fired pieces from sticking to the shelves. This preparation is far more important in ceramic firing at much higher temperatures. We do not use kiln wash on the shelves when firing painted glass with the painted side up. We do go to the precaution of preparing the shelves with wash when firing a silver-stained piece (which is fired stained side down), as well as when firing pieces that are painted on both sides.

Types of Kilns

We generally use an electric top-loading kiln to fire our painted pieces because we like to look in and see how they are doing. A front-loading kiln certainly works as well. Of course, you can go strictly by the pyrometer to tell when your pieces are done, or look through the peephole. Each kiln and pyrometer has its own idiosyncracies, which you will gradually become familiar with.

Normal firing of painted glass is done at about 1100°F. Tack firing, which is used in multiple firings of the same piece of glass, generally runs from 950°F to 1050°F. Once the proper firing temperature is reached, the kiln is turned off and allowed to cool. The problem is that it is very difficult to say when glass is fired to completion. That's why we like to look. Some painters say that

65

when the glass is the color of glowing liver it is ready. It rather depends on the glass. If the pieces get too red hot, the edges of the glass will round off and shrink back somewhat, making them too small for the leaded borders you have prepared. A very shiny painted surface on the cooled glass is also considered by many painters to be a sign of overfiring. Yet, if you don't fire enough, the paint won't fire in properly and will wear poorly.

Our feeling is that whatever type of kiln you use, you will have to acquaint yourself with its particular characteristics before you can really determine how your firings should proceed. We have found no difference in the way painted glass reacts to heat whether it be from a gas or electric kiln. The difference is more a matter of convenience to the worker.

One classic type of kiln for large studio use (though individual painters have employed them as well) is the flash kiln, in which the glass and the flame are in the same chamber. The flash kiln is very fast firing, which is most advantageous if you are doing a large amount of work. You can fire some flash kilns in 8 to 12 minutes, then move your glass out of the firing chamber to cool slowly in an adjacent area of the kiln. These kilns are expensive, and not many are made, but those that are last a long time.

Either bottle or regular gas may be used in a flash film. The gas jets are on the side of the firing chamber, tilted up toward the dome of the kiln. The glass pieces ride in an asbestos tray below them. The burners sweep the fire up to the crown of the kiln, instantly permeating the chamber with a high heat. The glass fires very readily. Flash kilns do not require a pyrometer. The worker goes by eye to reckon that the glass is done. The reason that the heat can be brought up so swiftly without cracking the glass is that the glass is so evenly heated in this type of arrangement. Cooling, however, is another matter. Many flash kilns have trays on racks which are then moved out to a slow cooling device.

Cooling the Glass

No matter how rapidly you fire it, glass should be cooled slowly. It's best to let the glass cool overnight with the electric kiln closed. By morning you can safely remove the pieces. If you want to push this process a bit you can do so by opening the top of your kiln directly after firing and watching the pyrometer very carefully. There is a crucial point down to which the glass can be cooled fairly rapidly. Most painted glass fires at around 1100°F. The critical point in cooling seems to be somewhere around 520°F. This is the point at which the silicate in the glass inverts to either an alpha or beta quartz. It is an area of expansion and if the cooling is too rapid here the glass will fragment. At this point you must close your kiln. Once this point is passed you can, again, cool the glass quickly by re-opening the kiln.

Many workers in full production have no time to wait out a long term cooling process and take the chance with fast cooling. It is a bit risky, though, and if you don't want to take any chances, we recommend slow cooling in a closed kiln. We have been purposely vague with the critical cooling point because you must experiment with your own kiln to find out exactly where it is. It should be near 520°F as we have indicated. You may find your glass will start to ping (the first indication of unbearable stress in the material) somewhere above or below that temperature. You may, in fact, find that your glass has no critical range but cools rapidly right down to a point where you can remove it from the kiln with no problems. The smaller the piece of glass, the more likely this is to happen. Large pieces, ones over 6" x 8", may break when you try this procedure on them. On the other hand you may be lucky. We have rapidly cooled pieces larger than 8" x 10" with no breakage occurring. We just open the top of the kiln and walk away from it. However, these heroic measures could, sooner or later, get you into trouble. It is much safer to watch for the critical zone; safer still to allow the glass to slow cool for the requisite length of time.

Multiple Firings

As you will see when we discuss double and triple matting, it is possible to fire a piece of painted glass many times. It is not necessary, or desirable, to think that firing it once finishes the job. There are painters that fire their piece of glass as many as six or seven times, each time for a different color, value, or stain. Occasionally the stain itself is multiple fired to vary its values.

Naturally you want each firing to do as much as possible, to combine as many different values or shadings as possible on one piece of glass. This can be done because the glass can be painted on two surfaces and still look as though only one surface was used. It is also made possible by using vehicles (which carry the color) that do not mix, so if you are careful you can paint over another vehicle's color without spoiling it.

It is your choice whether you wish to do multiple firings and fire in each value as it is done, rather than take the chance of disturbing an unfired color by painting over it with something else. Our feeling is that as you become more expert in your painting and develop more confidence in yourself and your materials, you will easily be able to combine several values of matt in one firing.

In multiple firings the glass must be cooled more slowly than one would cool it for a single firing. The stresses and strains that occur from a single firing within the piece of glass are multiplied by several firings and coolings. These stresses seem to take effect mostly during the cooling period when the coefficient of expansion of the glass is strained to its utmost.

All multiple firings need not go all the way up to the maximum firing temperature. A piece of glass can be tack fired—that is, only partly fired, perhaps 90 percent of the way up to maximum—so that while the paint does not totally imbed into the glass, it will adhere enough for your purposes. You can then paint your other color or stain on it when it has cooled. Once all your colors are applied, and each has been tack fired, you can then give the glass a final firing up to the proper firing temperature to make sure that all the paint will be permanent. In this manner you alleviate many of the potential problems inherent in firing the glass.

PART TWO

Trace Painting

✂ CHAPTER 7

Introduction to
Trace Painting

Tracing is the application of lines of graphic delineation, usually following a cartoon or pattern placed under the glass. These lines are usually applied with an opaque paint in a manner so that no light can come through them. Occasionally, some tracing lines are made more translucent, in which case they are called halftones. Halftones allow about a quarter or half the light to penetrate the line, rather than blocking it out entirely as is the case in most tracing.

Tracing can also be put on in a translucent manner, as in more realistic flesh painting. In such instances, it will allow through more light than does the typical halftone, and is utilized almost as a matt. All the same, it is applied with greater density than is the matt. At their most extreme, trace lines would be entirely opaque, matt entirely translucent; trace would block out light entirely; matt would modify the amount coming through in varying degrees. This does not mean that a tracing paint cannot be used as a matt paint or a matt paint cannot be used as a tracing paint. Nothing in the composition of either type of paint rules out its use in such a fashion. The confusion here lies in nomenclature, not physical properties.

*What Is
Tracing?*

We will start our tracing by working on a clean piece of window glass. (In fact, you'll find it helpful to have several clean pieces ready.) Make certain that the glass is clean, because impurities on its surface will interfere with your paint. Commercial window cleaners tend to leave a residue over the glass which can prevent the paint from adhering to it, cloud it up so you cannot see your underlying trace lines, or worse, add impurities that will show up after the glass has been fired. We've always found the best way to make sure a piece of glass is clean is to smear a little mixed paint on either surface and rub it around. The grittiness of the paint will make the glass bright and shiny for use. The amount of paint you waste doing this is inconsequential. Kiln wash will also do a good job. Wipe the glass with newspaper or a clean rag.

If you are dealing with scrap glass that has putty on it, try putting a handful of sodium phosphate in a pail of water. Be sure to use rubber gloves when handling this. Put the glass in the pail and

*Preparing Your
Materials*

let it stand for an hour or so—the old putty can then be easily scraped off.

With your glass clean, lay out the tracing brushes you intend to use. Each of three different sizes will be enough to begin with, and you may never need or want more than these. But you should become familiar with at least three. You will be practicing tracing initially without a cartoon (line drawing that is to be traced), but when the time comes to use one, make sure that it lies flat under the glass. You might want to cellophane tape it down so it doesn't move, although the weight of the glass should suffice. You won't need to work on a light table at this stage since you are working clear glass. You should, however, have plenty of light. Make sure your glass palette is clean and available.

Grinding Hancock Paints

For some reason an entire mystique has grown up around grinding paints, a simple (and mostly unnecessary) endeavor. It is only with the Hancock paints that you will even need your muller; all other standard paints have been ground for you. All paints need to be *mixed* (perhaps this is the confusing word), but only Hancock needs to be ground. Certainly today we should be able to dispense with this holdover excuse to give apprentices something to do. One of us, when an apprentice, was told to grind paint for eight hours. A whole day of grinding paint—alleviating any necessity of teaching for that time span.

Grinding, then, should be a word used only rarely today. If you are using a Hancock tracing color for this initial exercise, however, before you go any further you will have to grind the paint—Hancock's paints have a fairly large particle size and are quite gritty. For this you will need your glass muller and palette. Put however much of the dry paint you intend to use on the palette. Don't grind the entire contents of the envelope unless you are going to use it all. We suggest a full tablespoon (approximately one ounce) as a standard amount. Add gum and vehicle and grind this with your muller until all grittiness has disappeared and you have a uniform fine mix. This shouldn't take more than ten to fifteen minutes. Hancock paints, in our estimation, for all the work involved, are not as good for color and flow as are Drakenfeld paints.

Adding Gum Arabic

Gum arabic is a necessary, not an optional, ingredient for glass paint which has water or vinegar as a vehicle. We have never used trace or matt without some sort of binder being added, and gum is the usual one. There is no special effect we are aware of to justify not adding gum to your paint. The gum is a bonding agent between the paint and the vehicle and the glass. Without it your paint will not seem to have enough body to it. Without gum, the traced line tends to smudge and the matted area to wipe off. The trace line does not flow as well without it, nor does the matt blend satisfactorily.

Some painters add a little sugar or glycerine to the paint to retard the drying time of the vehicle and help the paint flow to an even depth in the painted line. This doesn't take the place of gum, but it will help give a more uniform look to the color. This technique is especially effective where you want a deep, dark color over a fairly large area of glass. This retarding of the drying process is only a physical aid to allow the color to disperse more readily over the area. It does nothing to it chemically, and it is no substitute for gum.

We have spent a considerable amount of time trying to work out an exact ratio of gum to paint since no one, to our knowledge, has ever come up with a satisfactory figure. Eventually the ratio that we developed was about one part gum to thirty-two parts paint. Most painters go by eye. However, without experience, your eye is quite liable to add too much or too little, leading to the common seesaw attempt at reconciliation by over-adding paint, then over-adding gum until you have a pile on your palette resembling Mount Everest.

One to thirty-two will work. Or you can use a pile of gum about ⅛ inch wide and high to two to three palette knives of paint, using the end of the palette blade to calculate from. Still another method is to sprinkle gum over the pile of paint so that it resembles a very light snowfall (figure 7-1). Obviously not a lot of gum is called for. Its presence in the mix, however small, is nonetheless essential.

Whether you use gum in powdered or liquid form doesn't seem to make any difference. We have experimented with both and both seem to do the job equally well. For the liquid we found that one measured tablespoon of paint would take $1/4$ measured teaspoon of 14 Baum strength liquid gum. This mixture comes out of the kiln with a smooth, uniform line (figure 7-2). Within the range of proportion above, keep in mind that the softer you want the trace or matt, the less gum you would add.

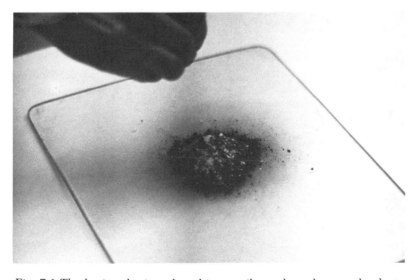

Fig. 7-1 The basic color is gathered into a pile on the palette, and a dusting of gum arabic is sprinkled over it.

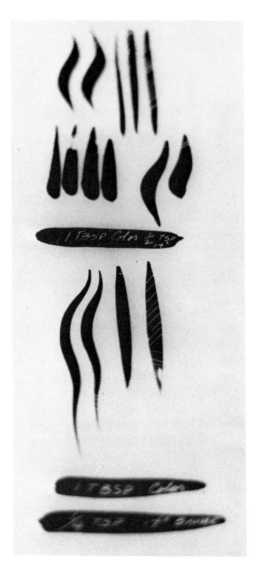

Fig. 7-2 Test firings for various mixes of paint and liquid gum arabic. The bottom color graded the best for consistency and ease of firing without frying. Note the test scratches in the above trace lines to check for resistance and chipping. The lower right vertical stroke has chipped at its lower pole—an indication of too much gum. Several other strokes also show signs of chipping.

Adding the Vehicle

We are going to use Drakenfeld tracing black #E-458. There are a number of good tracing blacks. Others with equally good consistency are Drakenfeld #401 and #2877. These seem to flow nicely, do not get too soft, and fire in well.

Pile an amount of paint in the center of your palette, add gum as indicated above (mix it dry—see figure 7-3), and with the tip of your spatula make a small hole in the middle of the pile (figure 7-4). Into this hole you are going to pour the vehicle, which can be either vinegar or water. We will use water to start.

WATER TRACE

Pour a little water into the hole you've scooped in the paint. Fold the sides of the hole into this center well of water so that as much of the paint as possible is initially exposed to moisture (figure 7-5). Once the water has pretty well permeated the pile of

Fig. 7-3 The gum and the color are mixed dry with the spatula to make them as homogeneous as possible.

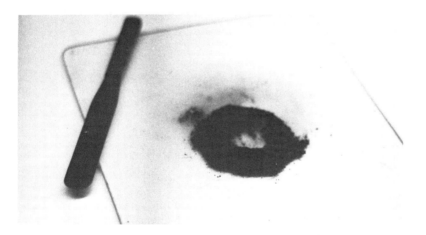

Fig. 7-4 A small recess in the center of the pile will receive the vehicle.

Fig. 7-5 Once the vehicle has been poured into the hole, the color is folded into the center to get as much of it exposed to the vehicle as possible.

paint, the mixing process (using your spatula, not your muller) can commence.

VINEGAR TRACE

Vinegar trace paint is the same paint we have been discussing, except it is mixed with vinegar instead of water. The vinegar should be fairly fresh. We have found a difference in the feel of the paint and the flow when stale vinegar is used. Naturally we are speaking here of white vinegar (we use Heinz), not wine vinegar—though wine has been used as a vehicle for painting, to say nothing of painters. Some beginners think the vinegar must be diluted with water. It need not be.

The vinegar gives a different flow to the paint than does water; the paint sort of gets a better "bite" on the glass. Some painters claim a smoother flow as well with vinegar rather than water. However, the main reason for using vinegar is to save a firing. Unfired vinegar trace will stick to the glass when it is matted over with the water matt, whereas water trace will smudge if matted over before firing. When water trace is used, the glass must be fired (tack fired, perhaps) and then the matt is applied over the fired trace lines. The piece is then fired again. If you were to matt over water trace paint with water matt without first firing the trace paint, soon the matt would smudge the trace lines and you would have a general mess. This does not happen when vinegar trace paint is used. The unfired vinegar trace remains where you put it despite matting over it.

Warning: Improper mixing, insufficient drying time, and humidity variations can contribute to unfired vinegar trace failing to adhere when water matt is applied over it. It is wise to use an economy of strokes when blending matt over unfired vinegar trace, as excessive activity can penetrate its resistance to water.

It is a little scary at first to apply matt over unfired trace. It is, however, a good technique to master. Aside from saving time by eliminating a firing, it allows for a certain flexibility in that you can work up a more complete statement with trace and matt without having to commit yourself to an obligatory firing interlude. We will have more to say about this technique when we talk about matting.

Vinegar trace also tends to give somewhat better control of half-tones (lines that are only semi-opaque) than does water trace. Depending on your mixture you can get a deep black to a translucent gray line much more easily with vinegar than with water. However, not all painters agree on this and, in any event, that alone would not be the basic reason for choosing vinegar over water.

Vinegar trace paint does have certain disadvantages. First of all, it has a very pungent odor which is unpleasant to some people. More important, it is affected more by the vagaries of the weather than water paint seems to be. Vinegar trace paint still uses gum arabic, just as does water paint.

We suggest that you first get acquainted with water trace and after you have developed a certain familiarity with it, then do some experimenting with vinegar trace. Fire up some of the lines and exercises you have done with both and compare them. Check for opacity and halftones. The essential choice of any vehicle is for its applicability to the work in hand. Many vehicles have been used in order to achieve some idiosyncrasy peculiar to them. Our purpose here, however, is not to get into esoteric particulars, but to develop in you a painting ability.

Mixing and Piling Up the Paint

Having added your gum and water, you now take your spatula and begin to mix your paint. It is not quite as simple as it sounds. The idea is to mix, not displace. First, the spatula must be held correctly, in direct contact with the pile of paint (see figure 7-6). You must also lift the edge of your spatula occasionally to gather more fresh paint and release what has already been mixed (figure 7-7). Keeping the blade of the spatula flat, as shown in the top of figure 7-6, and making circular motions over and over isn't proper mixing. You will only re-mix those grains that have happened to get under the spatula. The rest of the stuff will only be pushed around. You can do this all day long and not really mix the paint. To make your motions count and accomplish something, you must move your wrist as you move your spatula and hold the spatula at a changeable angle so that you are constantly gathering new paint under it and forcing it between the blade and the glass surface. Only in this manner will you get a good mix.

In figures 7-8 and 7-9 we have attempted to show routes of the spatula as it circles through the paint. We have found that mixing is best accomplished when a specific pattern is followed as there is less likelihood that a portion of the paint will be left out. If you just keep stirring the same area over and over, or choose areas at random, chances are you will stir around the same areas of paint while overlooking others. You can switch back and forth from one pattern to the next. This will pretty much guarantee all the paint getting mixed thoroughly and will cut down the mixing time considerably.

Watching a good glass painter mix paint is like watching a good dancer. There is the same sense of rhythm and lissomeness. It is this motion that you should seek to develop. Like everything else in glass painting, it takes practice. But, like everything else, once you get it down, you will never forget it—and you will be able to do the job in hand with grace and precision.

Don't be afraid to add water to your paint as you mix (figure 7-10). Add it a little bit at a time as it is needed. If you add too much, just pour it off and keep mixing until the remainder of the excess evaporates. Don't add more paint; chances are you will over-compensate and then have to add more water and more gum—and pretty soon you'll have enough paint to do the house. The paint mixture should achieve a certain consistency—the best way we can describe this is to compare it to stirred yogurt. When your

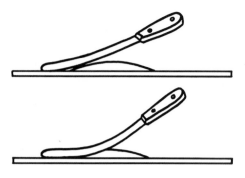

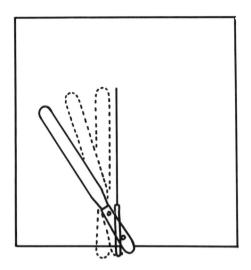

Fig. 7-6 The spatula must be held at an angle so it will stir as much paint as possible per stroke. Incorrect position (top): the spatula is barely touching the pile of paint, and mixing, no matter how energetic, will be inefficient. Correct position (bottom): The spatula is directly contacting the paint and can move around large portions of it.

Fig. 7-7 Positions of the spatula in mixing, from flat to the palette to an angle of approximately 90°. During the mixing process the spatula keeps rising and flattening, guided by the wrist, so as to constantly gather fresh paint under the surface of the blade.

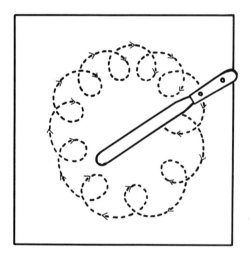

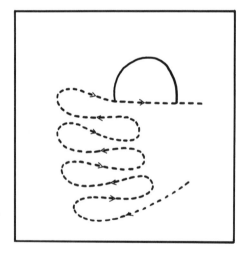

Fig. 7-8 In addition to the spatula blade lifting up and down, it travels around the palette to mix all the paint that is there.

Fig. 7-9 Alternate mixing pattern. This one goes from side to side.

paint is well mixed and is the right consistency, you will pile it all together in the center of your palette and get it ready to work with (figure 7-12).

Piled paint is paint that has been arranged in the most effective manner for the glass painter to utilize. A reservoir of color is held in a pile toward the back of the palette. The front of the pile, facing

Fig. 7-10 Small amounts of water are added as necessary.

Fig. 7-11 The mixing process continues in the center of the palette.

the painter, leads to a little well of color and vehicle where the paint is mixed by the brush as it is being loaded. Moist color from the front of the pile is drawn into the well as needed, to be mixed with vehicle to the proper consistency for painting (figures 7-13 and 7-14).

You will be adding brushfulls of water to the well, as well as paint from the reservoir, in order to keep the color constant. If the color is too dry, it will be prone to drag rather than flow. In this case, you would add water (if water is your vehicle) until the consistency is appropriate. If the paint is too wet, it will be hard to

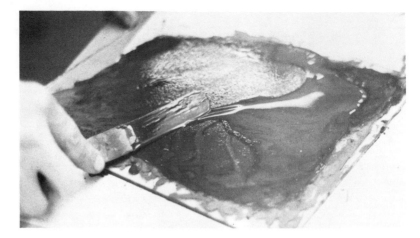

Fig. 7-12 The final step in preparing color is to gather it into a pile or reservoir.

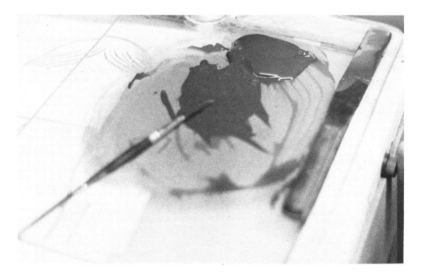

Fig. 7-13 This is the end result of a good mix of trace. The paint reservoir is toward the back of the palette; the well (the mixing area where working consistency is achieved) spreads over the center of the palette.

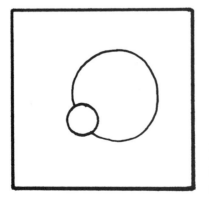

Fig. 7-14 Diagram of the trace palette. The larger circle represents the reservoir or pile of paint; the smaller circle is the well.

control and will have a tendency to run as well as to produce half-tones where it should be opaque. To correct this, more color would be brought down from the reservoir into the well.

Adding Color or Gum to the Pile

Before you attempt any painting check to see that your paint is the correct consistency. Test the resistance of a few dry trace lines by running the back of your brush handle over them lightly. Gum tends to flow to the sides of the line, not clump up in the center, so you will normally have some resistance at the sides. Resistance, however, should be slight. If the cross lines your brush handle makes through the paint lines are clean and the resistance is minimal, your paint is probably all right. However, if the line chips or flakes as you enter it with the back of your paint brush, you have too much gum and the line will likely fry in the firing. In this case, you will want to dilute the excess gum by adding more color. In some instances, you may find the painted line indicates a lack of gum. You then must add some.

Never dump dry gum or color directly into the already-mixed paint. If you do this, you are liable to get lumps and have great difficulty integrating the mix. The only way to add gum or color to the basic pile of mixed paint is to mix the gum or color with water or vinegar to a proper consistency and then add it to the mixed pile of paint. Then test it again with new trace lines.

Positioning

Tracing is done "down" at the light table. You may practice without using a light table initially, but eventually, even if you are using clear window glass, you are going to have to get the practice of using backlighting. Very few painters trace up on an easel and those that do have developed a very personal technique which may work well for them but would not necessarily work well for anyone else. We do not recommend it.

Most painters stand during the tracing process because it is easier to work over the bridge this way. We find there is better control of the brush stroke when one stands rather than sits. Have some sort of rug or mat to stand on if your feet tire easily. We have found that the process of painting is so fascinating that one doesn't notice the time going by and before you know it you have been standing for several hours at a stretch. Your legs might resent it if they go this long in one position. Of course, you can interrupt your work, walk about, or sit down if you wish, but we bet you'll be so wrapped up in your painting, you will forget about everything else.

Using the Bridge

We want to discuss the employment of the bridge before talking about using the tracer per se. This is because too many students think that the bridge is strictly a subsidiary item. Unfortunately, some of the quick paint books that have recently come out have promulgated this impression to the detriment of anyone who attempts any painting by such methods. In fact, you cannot do any substantial tracing without knowing how to use the bridge. This simple but particular tool can make the difference between substantial accomplishment or continuous frustration. Trace painting should not be done without a bridge, except in very special instances.

To begin with, the bridge is not a hand rest. It is an equal partner in the tracing activity, as important in its way as the tracer and your hand. Its use involves a precise technique which, while it may seem a trifle awkward at first, will pay off later in a more efficient productivity. If you use the bridge wrongly, however, it can end up crippling your efforts, rather than enhancing them.

The following suggestions will help you utilize the bridge more effectively:

1. The bridge should be held approximately parallel to the line you are tracing. This provides for maximum use of its surface as both a guide and a rest for the working hand. As you follow the line down, your hand should be balanced along its heel.

2. It is the heel of the hand that provides the fulcrum for most of the tracing done from the bridge. The fingers and wrist revolve around this point area.

3. Try not to lift the heel of your hand off the bridge. Initially you may have to fight this tendency. If any lifting of the hand becomes necessary to follow a particular line, the front part of the hand can lift up or down (if a curve is to be accomplished or more pressure on the brush is required), but the heel should remain stable on the bridge.

4. Hold the bridge from the bottom; that is, the working hand should almost always be above the holding hand (this is shown in figure 9-9). The tendency of many students is to hold the bridge from the top. This puts one hand in the other's way, and the upper hand will limit the types of strokes you will be able to do. It will also limit your ability to see what is going on above the working hand. In addition, there is a decided tendency to lean on the bridge when the holding hand is above the work hand. The bridge is not meant for support. It is a functional object and serves its purpose best when held from below. Keep close watch on yourself in this regard.

5. You can use the bridge as a template for certain designs—as in the employment of its straight edge as a direct guide for the tracer. This is very effective in providing straight or parallel lines, though you must remember to maintain the proper pressure of the brush against the glass to keep the breadth of line the same. Be sure the bridge edge is smooth and even.

6. Where you place the bridge when tracing specific designs can have an effect on your work. We will be giving suggestions as to bridge placement in the tracing exercises in the following chapter.

7. Remember to make the best use of the natural arch of your hand which is poised on the bridge some distance above the work. This allows a greater range of movement than if your hand were resting directly on the glass.

8. You may sometimes have to move the bridge to a different

position to complete a stroke. Although it is not always possible to accomplish every stroke within the range of a single bridge and hand position, we suggest that you try to get as much mileage out of each stroke as possible, and, if you have to leave a stroke in the middle and move the bridge to a different position to finish it, take the stroke up at that point and try to complete the line in as few strokes as possible.

9. The bridge should be held close enough to trace the line so that the tracer forms almost a right angle with the glass. If the bridge is too far away from the trace line, you will find yourself awkwardly stretching with your brush.

Basic hand position on the bridge is shown in figure 7-15. Notice that the bridge is held parallel to the line of work. The hand rests on the heel, angled to get the maximum wrist and finger mobility. The tracer is held securely but not in a pinched fashion. The

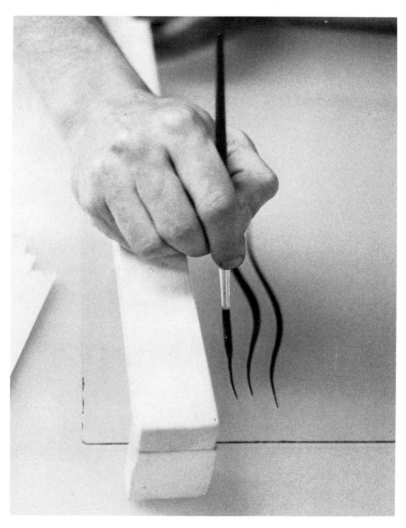

Fig. 7-15 Basic hand position on the bridge. Almost any shaped line can be traced in this fashion.

bridge is positioned so the tracer is at almost right angles to the glass. With a slight motion of the wrist, the pressure on the brush can be increased or decreased to accomplish thick or thin strokes or a combination of these within the same line as is shown here.

The bridge is a handmaiden to your wrist, arm, and fingers, and it should help, not inhibit, you. You can, as we pointed out, move it around. While you shouldn't have to move it all over the place, neither should you try to make your tracing fit the bridge. Use the bridge in a manner most comfortable for you. It may be difficult at first to discover just which is the most comfortable position for various endeavors, but you'll be surprised how fast you'll get used to it. And, as you get more secure with the bridge, you'll find your tracing strokes become more precise. Please, however, remember to hold the bridge from the bottom. The sooner you get used to doing this, the better.

Loading the Brush

You will now have in front of you your tracing brush, a cup of water, the mix of paint and vehicle piled on your palette (this pile will be referred to as the reservoir), your bridge, and a piece of clear window glass on which you will practice some strokes.

Start by loading your tracing brush with paint. There is a definite technique to loading the brush. This is accomplished by first dipping your tracer into the water to separate the hairs and then into the well of paint and vehicle at the foot of the reservoir. Do not load the brush from the color reservoir directly. You draw the color to the little well of mix in front of the reservoir and swirl the hairs around in the well, drawing needed color from the reservoir (figure 7-16).

Fig. 7-16 Loading the brush. Swirl it about in the well of color so that all bristles pick up paint.

The idea is to get a brushful of paint, not a tipful. Tracing brushes are specifically shaped to be able to hold quite a deal of paint without running out in the middle of a stroke. Make sure you get some paint into the back portion of the brush, which is the reserve from which the paint runs down to the tip. If this back portion stays dry, then you will run out of paint rather abruptly. When loaded, draw the brush across the palette to get back the proper shape of the hairs and the most workable placement of paint within the brush.

At this point, if you hold the brush horizontally in front of you, you should be able to see quite readily what its particular "set" is; that is, which is the top and which the bottom so far as the hairs of the brush are concerned. The hairs will take on a rounded surface for the bottom and a flatter surface for the top. Turn the brush slowly in front of you to determine this set. Determining just which is top and which is bottom for the particular brush in hand will give you the optimal working surface for this brush, and you can then employ it to its fullest capacity.

If you do not make certain to twirl your brush in the mix of paint and vehicle in the well in front of the reservoir, the vehicle and the color will not mix properly in the brush, and instead of nice opaque lines you will start getting halftones. This can be from either too much or too little vehicle (water) preventing the color from flowing. Halftones do not necessarily mean a lack of sufficient color in the reservoir. Unfortunately some workers assume halftones mean just that and start adding ingredients to their basic mix. All this does is compound the problem. Don't be in a hurry to add substances to the reservoir once you have it mixed and tested. First

Fig. 7-17 Lifting the brush from the color. All the bristles are loaded evenly with paint. Note how the brush dips downward.

check that the ingredients that are already there are still mixed together correctly to the proper consistency.

A brush should be fully loaded, but it should not be overloaded. Paint should flow from the brush in a continuous manner, but there should be no blob of paint gathering at the tip of the hairs. This will only blot the glass and serve to ruin most of what you have already done. The point should remain sharp, with a reservoir of paint at the heel of the brush. This paint then moves down through the tracer in a sort of capillary action, renewing the paint at the tip of the brush as it is applied to the glass. Control of the amount of paint that ends up on the glass is through the pressure of your hand and wrist and fingers guiding the brush.

Always test stroke the brush on the palette to make sure there is no excess of color to blob in case the brush has become overloaded. This will also give you an idea how smoothly your color is flowing and how good your mix is. Should you accidentally overload the brush with paint, the best thing to do is to twirl the brush in a spiraling manner across the palette to remove the excess and work with what remains (figure 7-18).

Using the Tracing Brush

Some individuals are daunted by the long-haired tracing brush and dab with it rather than stroke. The basic tracing stroke utilizes the potential of your entire arm. It can begin with the fingers, move to the wrist, and then bring in the forearm or just the opposite, depending on the character of the line. It is necessary to exhaust the potential of each member before getting into the next. Not all trace strokes will utilize all your arm. Some will call only for finger involvement, whereas long flowing lines may em-

Fig. 7-18 Working excess color from the brush.

ploy only forearm strokes. We will show you what we mean with the exercises in the following chapter.

You will begin your trace painting with a wide-open sort of exercise, though not an undisciplined one. The painting strokes should be practiced initially without any cartoon to follow so you can get the feel of the tracer and what it can accomplish. Starting off with freehand strokes (using the bridge!) rather than following a cartoon will allow you to develop a sense of spontaneity rather than the restrictiveness many beginners feel when they first pick up a tracer.

Don't be annoyed with yourself if you don't get the proper consistency of paint in your lines right off. Concentrate on moving the tracer around, loading it, and reloading it with paint. As you progress, your lines will become more what you think trace lines should look like. Hold your tracing brush with about the same pressure as you hold a pencil, and at an angle to the glass as indicated in figure 7-19.

Concentrate on getting comfortable with the bridge. Do not use the bridge as an arm rest or hold it at right angles to a brush stroke, no matter how much easier it may seem, because the bridge can't do much for you in this position.

Start off with a series of straight lines using the bridge as a guide for the line (figure 7-21). As the tracer travels the length of the bridge, it is important to keep the same amount of pressure on it so that the trace line will remain at an equal width throughout. This is one technique where the bridge may be held from the top,

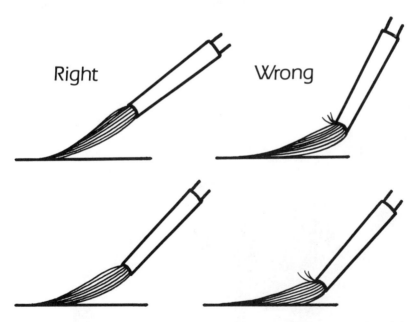

Fig. 7-19 Right and wrong tracing brush angle. Wrong: Note that the angle between handle and hairs is so great that hairs are broken by the ferrule. Right: The angle between the ferrule and the hairs is not extreme.

as shown in the pictures. Try drawing parallel lines (figure 7-22) both using the bridge as a guide and holding the brush away from the bridge with just your arm as a guide.

Now do some lines, remembering to exhaust the potential of the bridge position before moving it. You'll be surprised how far your wrist can pivot on the heel of your hand to get that arc traced on the glass without having to move the bridge at all. Figures 7-23 through 7-25 illustrate tracing an arc by pivoting the hand on the bridge.

Flowing lines are a wrist/arm exercise. Hold the bridge from the bottom and parallel to the brush stroke so it is an integral part of producing the flow of line. Figures 7-26 through 7-33 show the tracing of free-flowing curved lines.

Practice putting different amounts of pressure on the brush to see how thick and how thin you can make your lines. Impart a little swirl to your lines, and do some long S-shaped trace lines. As you apply varying degrees of pressure to your tracing brush, you will, of course, see the hairs dip downward and splay a bit or rise up until only the tip touches the glass, creating lines that vary from thick to thin or thin to thick. Some find it is easier to go from thick to thin while some people find the opposite the case, so don't consider yourself particularly awkward if you find this a bit of a problem at first. Just keep practicing strokes with particular emphasis on those portions that you feel least comfortable with.

It's a good idea to have several practice pieces of clear glass on hand so that when you have painted lines all over one, you can immediately continue practicing on the next. And remember not to waste paint. When you have filled up one practice glass, don't wash away the paint. Take a razor blade and scrape all the used paint onto a spare piece of glass. You can later remix this and add

Fig. 7-20 This raccoon shows a clever use of parallel traced lines on the tail to save lead lines. *Courtesy of Helena Kedda.*

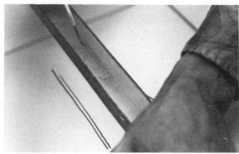

Fig. 7-21 In straight line tracing, the side of the bridge may be used as a guide. The work hand guides the tracer down the side of the bridge, applying constant pressure, to produce a very straight, even line.

Fig. 7-22 Parallel lines being drawn as part of straight line tracing practice.

Fig. 7-23 Positioning the hand for tracing an arc is somewhat awkward at first. Note how the bridge is held parallel to the stroke. Here we show how holding the hand at right angles to the stroke limits the ability to do the arc in one graceful stroke. Instead, to start the stroke, the wrist should be held parallel to the bridge.

Fig. 7-24 The angle of the hand at the conclusion of the arc stroke. The conclusion of the stroke is mostly a finger motion, the brush being tucked under the palm as it goes toward the bridge. Much of the tucking under is due to the pressure of the index finger taking up where wrist movement leaves off.

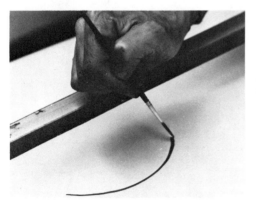

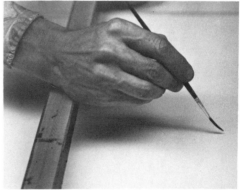

Fig. 7-25 Another view of the stroke, showing the tucked under position of the brush. The arc has been done in one stroke, which is the main purpose of the exercise.

Fig. 7-26 Free-flowing lines start with the wrist at right angles to the bridge to reach the furthest point of the line. A single stroke is required, not a combination of strokes.

Note: In figures 7-24 through 7-32, the bridge is placed correctly at right angles to the body, not parallel to it.

Fig. 7-27 The beginning stroke being pulled with finger motion back toward the bridge.

Fig. 7-28 The finger motion is now more advanced and the wrist starts to roll to bring the stroke parallel to the bridge.

Fig. 7-29 The roll of the wrist is becoming more evident as the stroke takes on a new direction.

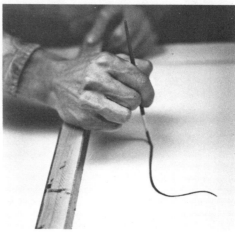

Fig. 7-30 Note the change in hand and finger position as the wrist moves down the bridge carrying the trace line along.

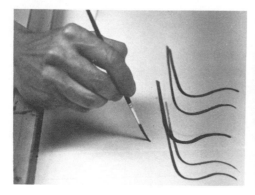

Fig. 7-31 Several practice strokes have been completed. Once again there is that reach out to start another curve.

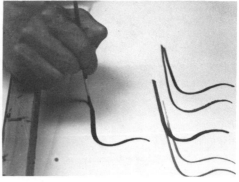

Fig. 7-32 A variance of pressure will make the same curve go from thin to thick.

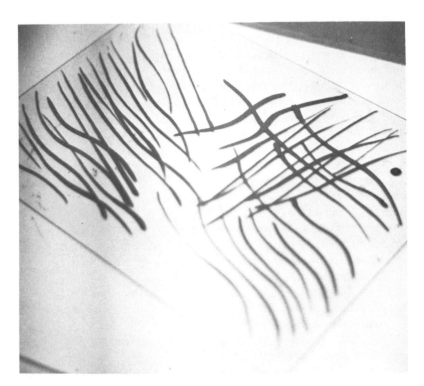

Fig. 7-33 Practice tracing free-flowing lines in all directions, using the bridge. Don't worry about the aesthetics of the thing; just have a ball.

it back to your working pile. Don't add it to the pile directly, but mix it up with a little water (you won't need to add more gum), and when it is the proper consistency, put it back to use. This way you can use the same paint over and over as you practice without any waste.

As you practice your tracing strokes, you'll be getting used to several things at once: paint flow, the tracer, the bridge, and moving your arm, wrist, and fingers. It can be a little awkward at first, but we've all gone through it. You may hold the brush too tightly so that your wrist shakes; you may hold it so loosely that it falls from your hand. You will be getting alternately thick and thin lines from varying pressure, even where you don't want them.

It is a lot to take in all at once, but you should find it fun. Don't worry about fine tracing; don't worry about sloppy lines. Make mistakes. You will get halftones, broken lines, all sorts of problems. That's fine. You aren't running a race, you know. Enjoy the learning process. As you keep practicing, you will be pleased to see how you begin to progress. You will start to develop a "hand sense" that will automatically tell you how much pressure to apply to the tracer to widen the line just a little, or a lot; or how much pressure to release so that you are using just the tip for a thin line. You will soon get accustomed to the bridge and appreciate its usefulness, and you will be able to accomplish your trace lines with sureness and dexterity.

Improvement, however, is a flighty thing. You may show a great amount of improvement all of a sudden and then not be able to attain that high standard again for a couple of hours—or even a couple of days. Rest assured, however, that it will return. It likes to tease you. Your hand, wrist, and arm, together with your budding skill, will come together and fall asunder repeatedly until finally you will have all the elements coordinated and wonder why you found any of this difficult in the first place.

Two cautions about practicing this lesson. Some students want to start a step further back and try to get the "feel" of their tracer against the glass without paint. This is a waste of time. You should not use a tracing brush without paint; get used to it in its functional state right away without "preparing to prepare."

The second caution is fatigue. We all get tired. When we do, we make more mistakes, get irritable, and tend to blame what we are doing. Be reasonable about your practicing. No matter how intrigued you become with learning to trace, as soon as you feel yourself getting up-tight, take a break. Getting away from what you are doing, if only for a few minutes, will allow you to approach it again with a fresh attitude and sharpened perspective. Don't worry about how fast someone else told you they learned (most people tend to exaggerate their facility in any event). Time is not important—results are! Once you find you are spending time that is not rewarding in any way, that your lines are regressing instead of progressing—go do something else. When you come back and renew your tracing, you will be amazed to find how frequently improvement has occurred.

Halftones and Other Imperfections

After you have painted lines for a while, you will want to hold your glass up to the light and see what they look like, since that is really the only way to tell. You might be a little dismayed to find they are mostly halftones—lines that are only semi-opaque. Either you do not have enough color on your brush, or the paint has not been mixed adequately in your well. Don't be terribly concerned about this at first. You can't be absolute about everything right away. The idea of this initial session is to get your hand in proper motion, not to paint a masterpiece.

Halftones are the usual error and the usual frustration of beginning painters. Even advanced painters have problems with them if they get careless. But don't assume that all halftones are accidents. An artist may create a halftone purposely, getting the reading of light he wishes through the use of a partially transparent line.

However, what we are more concerned with are lines that you intend to be jet black, completely blocking out the light, and which, while appearing opaque on the table, reveal their deceptive nature when held up to the light. What do you do about them? Well, one thing you should *not* do is take your tracing brush and paint over the halftones in an attempt to make them more opaque. Adding trace paint in this fashion, while it may seem to improve matters initially, may be a disaster later on when you go to fire your doctored lines. They will tend to fry—that is, bubble up, curl, and char in the kiln as the disparate layers of paint twist apart from the heat.

The best thing to do with halftones is to get rid of them—scrape them off your glass with a razor blade, mix your paint more thoroughly, and try again. You need not sacrifice your whole painting, of course. If only one or two lines in a tracing are too light, scrape these off and redo them. There's nothing wrong with salvaging what you can—we all do it.

Remember that pure black lines are seldom perfect, and rarely as opaque as you would wish them to be. However, continually practicing the proper pressure of the brush against the glass and getting the feel of correctly mixed paint will eventually result in your lines achieving a satisfactory opacity.

Other difficulties may arise in the course of a stroke. You may find little specks in the line where the paint has not taken. This could be due to a faulty brush stroke, poor filling of the brush with paint, paint that is too dry to flow properly, or dirt on the glass. In any event, there you are with all these little pinholes. Probably the best thing to do in the course of practice is try to find out which of the above reasons caused them, alleviate the problem, and do the lines over.

If you are painting something as a final step and pinholes occur, however, you will have to fill them in. Try to do this touching up while the paint is still wet or at least damp. The larger the area you have to touch up, the more important this becomes. If you put wet paint on top of dry paint, when you go to fire it, it will probably fry. Very small pinholes can be touched up, even if the paint has dried somewhat, but be careful not to blob the fresh paint about. It is disconcertingly easy to do this. Blobs of paint, aside from covering too much area to fire well, tend to have a little nipple of excess color in the center when you lift the brush. All around this area the paint will fry.

All you need in touching up is a dot. If you need more than just a dot here, a dot there, it is no longer a touching up job—it is a restoration. And that is another thing entirely. All touch-ups should be done not only lightly but very selectively, using just enough paint to obliterate the light that is coming through the pinhole. In most instances you can do this with the glass raised toward a light source, the brush posed to gently dot and fill in the discrepancy.

Don't get in the habit of painting carelessly just because you know you can make up the difference later. Every line you do should be traced as if there was no way to fix it. Keep this in mind; then, afterwards, when you lift your glass up to the light, if the whole thing is bad, you will quickly realize you have to scrape it off and do it again. But if most of it looks pretty good, with just a few imperfections, or just one or possibly two halftones, it is perfectly legal to scrape away the halftone lines and redo just those, as well as touching up pinholes with the point of the brush.

Excess water can be another problem. If you are painting along and you start having trouble with the paint not flowing properly, or if you start getting halftones and draggy halftones at that, the tendency is almost always to add too much water. Remember to add water only a little at a time. If your paint becomes watery, you won't be able to control it at all—it will run out from what should be a clean brush stroke all over the glass. Don't add more paint to the pile at this point, because you will probably compound the problem. Wait for the excess water to evaporate (which can seem like hours). The best thing is not to allow this to happen—make sure your paint is mixed well, and add very small amounts of water, if necessary, bit by bit.

If a tracer should skip while you are in the middle of a stroke (that is, if it doesn't give you a firm paint line on the glass surface) and you cannot find any reason for it behaving this way, the brush may not be at its proper set. All the hairs may not be contacting the glass surface to the brush's optimum effect. You might try turning the brush in your hand to get this individual instrument's most effective positioning. Brushes, like painters, are by no means all alike. Also, remember that oxhair and sable brushes paint quite differently. If you keep having trouble of this nature, you might want to try a brush of a different hair.

Practice Makes Imperfect

It may sound strange to say that practice makes you less perfect rather than more, but it all depends on how you look at it. Of course, the more you practice, the more adept you will become—and probably less satisfied with your work. Your demands will escalate ahead of your technique; you will suddenly find your criticism expanding, but your strokes still undernourished. One day you trace absolutely up to par; ten minutes later you'll find your new-found function back in the basement. It is frustrating—but it is all part of the learning process. Tracing, of all painting techniques, especially demands coordination and discipline of all portions of the body involved. This includes your eyes, fingers, wrist, arm—even the way you stand. Try to find a posture that you are comfortable with and get your arm used to moving from this standard balance. This is one of the things many beginners have trouble with—they stand differently each time. Any suddenly introduced twist of your body that wasn't there yesterday can make your today's painting a whole different scene.

Each day, or each session you have at your table, review briefly some of what you previously learned. You may find you haven't really learned it yet and your session may wind up being a total recapitulation of last session's work. This is all right up to a point—however, don't become so enamored of perfecting one particular stroke that you never get beyond it. One of our students spent an entire course seeking the Essence of the straight line. He was still practicing straight lines when the rest of the class was on the flower, when they were on the head, when they were on diapering, when they had completed the course. He is still, so far as we know, practicing his straight lines. Obviously this is the opposite extreme from the more typical student who wants to rush through all the initial practicing and immediately paint a Meyer-Munich or a Tiffany head by the second session. Our advice: make haste slowly, but don't stagnate.

We don't usually have to worry about students dragging along. If anything, many students show an impatience to get through basic exercises. This is regrettable. A certain amount of repetition is essential to any teaching process. Where physical control is the point at issue, repetition of strokes, pressures, turns and any other motions involved is not only part of the painting process, it *is* the painting process—without which creativity cannot be expressed. The value of disciplined practice is inestimable. At the end you will have completed works that embody fundamental principles of glass painting as well as creative self-expression.

✥ CHAPTER 8

Tracing Exercises: Finger Movements

In painting free-flowing strokes over a wide section of glass (chapter 7) you presumably have gotten used to the brush, to the S motion of your wrist and fingers, and to keeping the heel of your hand on the bridge. You have started to learn to minimize brush strokes, to make one take the place of two. If you have not yet been able to make a flowing S stroke with one swoop of the brush, with variance of the line between thick and thin, you should continue to practice this. These long strokes also will give your arm and wrist a sense of spontaneity which will be evident in the finished product.

Having started with these wide, open movements, we are now going to move on to the other extreme. Finger movements are tighter, smaller strokes. In order to introduce you to this motion, we have provided some specific exercises, which we will describe rather carefully, making general remarks and specific observations as we go along. Consider that you are in a classroom; that not everyone comprehends the same thing at the same time; that a certain amount of repetition is necessary.

You should practice all the finger movements, not just those which are easiest for you. Each of these exercises has grown out of a problem our students have had at one time or another, and you are the recipient of the various solutions we have found. If you do not have the particular problem, fine. Repetition of the exercise will make certain you won't have that particular problem in the future. We advise that after practicing these exercises individually, you combine a few of them. For example, take some of the curved lines and a circle to make an eye, or some of the wavy lines to do hair. Practice fine lines and thick lines; then combine both of them in C curves to make an ear. In this way you are continually putting together and breaking down the basic finger movements of trace painting.

Finger movement exercises emphasize the use of the fingers; it doesn't mean you cannot use the wrist as well. Generally, you won't have to use the arm with these exercises. Finger movements are important in tracing, and a good grounding in them is essential. The more precise you become with this type of motion, the more effective will be your result.

Use the bridge in finger movements as an extension of your

hand. Suggested bridge positions are provided with these exercises, and we recommend you try our suggestion before placing your bridge elsewhere. We didn't come by these selections arbitrarily; in each exercise we had students place their bridges in other positions, only to find the ones given here to be the most advantageous. Try not to move the bridge around excessively. These exercises, unlike the flowing lines already practiced, involve only minimal wrist motion and little, if any, arm motion. There should be no reason, therefore, for the bridge to be moved during a stroke nor for each stroke not to be completed as an entity, rather than being broken up into two. There are exceptions to this which we will consider at the appropriate time.

Vary your tracing brushes during these exercises. It is all too easy to get used to one brush, especially with finger work. Learn to use your small tracer even when you think a larger or thicker one will do a quicker job. On the other hand, it is not necessarily a good idea to use a very thick tracer when your thinner one might seem the more reasonable. Here you are only fighting your materials—always a losing battle. We want you to develop a good "hand sense" but common sense must also be used in these practice sessions.

These exercises are not a comprehensive survey of all the motions fingers use in trace painting, but they are a good introduction. We have divided them into groups, and we urge you to practice each group before going on to the next. Don't expect to get everything perfect right away. Use the entire surface of your clear glass, then scrape off the dry paint, as we have previously discussed, and go back to your practice.

When painting any of these exercises, or when tracing any line that can be accomplished with one stroke, it is not advisable or necessary to outline the edges of the area and then fill in between as you might do if you were painting a door, or a window, or working in other types of painting such as oils or watercolor. Try to get the complete line in one stroke. This is not always possible, of course, but it is always good discipline to make the effort. When more than one stroke is required, don't use a thin brush to trace the main outline and then switch to a thicker brush to put in the center portion of paint. To paint wide lines, use a thick brush to begin with, and you will be able to produce most of the width of the line in one stroke. Then, while what you have painted is still wet, take another stroke to fill in the rest of the line.

Exceptions, of course, always exist and if what you are painting requires many strokes to fill it, then you will have to outline. The problem with outlining is that by the time you are painting the center portion, your outline may be dry. The wet center impinging on these lines is liable to cause frying at these points. If you have to outline, therefore, use as thick a brush as possible so as to cover as much area as possible. Then when you go to paint the center, you will be able to meet up with the outline more rapidly.

Covering area rapidly and avoiding halftones and frying is what this type of tracing is all about. Where very wide areas are involved, a drop of glycerine mixed in your paint reservoir will help retard drying and allow the paint to spread to a uniform level within the painted lines. One drop of glycerine off the end of your paintbrush handle is all you need.

We suggest that you pencil trace the four accompanying illustrations as precisely as possible onto several sheets of paper. Then ink them up and use these sheets as cartoons under your glass. We do not recommend attempting to duplicate these figures from the book by working freehand in paint. This may prove quite frustrating since you will not have a direct guide. Do not attempt to put your glass over the book page and trace that way. All glass, to be painted on adequately, should be flat on a surface; the book is too unstable and you will just be wasting your time. Be smart; do it right the first time.

While doing these exercises it is easy to get so involved with bridge placement and brush strokes that you forget about keeping your paint at its proper consistency. Keep a small cup of water on hand. During tracing, one generally replaces the evaporated vehicle by dipping the tracing brush in the water (or vinegar). This motion will rapidly become second nature with you.

If your trace lines are shaky at first, rest assured that practice will overcome this. Don't feel inhibited. Don't demand perfection. A certain spontaneity will begin to appear as you continue with your painting and the shakiness will disappear. Try not to be overcautious at first. You aren't painting the Sistine Chapel, after all. Don't worry at this stage whether lines meet precisely or not. If one line overlaps another, let it go. As you keep practicing, you will get these lines to start and stop where you want them to.

Remember to employ to the utmost your major tool—the human hand. The arch of the hand pivoting on the heel gives your fingers and wrist the nimbleness to do their job, and a natural flow to the paint line. Try to develop a certain rhythm in your movements. Don't speed up or slow down in the same stroke. Many beginners start off very carefully on a line and then, as they go along, their eye and hand somehow get ahead of the brush and the line finishes in a rush that puts it out of control. As you improve you will take some pride in your trace lines terminating where you want them to end, not where the brush slips away from you.

Exercise One: Geometric Shapes

In figure 8-1, six geometrical designs are shown. Dotted lines indicate bridge placement. The bridge should be held parallel to the dotted lines, not necessarily on top of them. Dotted lines also indicate a center of balance and direction of the figures, to help you relate to them spatially. The dotted lines do *not* indicate the center of the bridge. Please bear this in mind.

Shape 1 shows two crossed lines of moderate thickness with blunt ends. Your medium or small tracer should accomplish this. Use the edge of your bridge as a guide; you will position the bridge twice as indicated. One object of this exercise is to attain the blunt

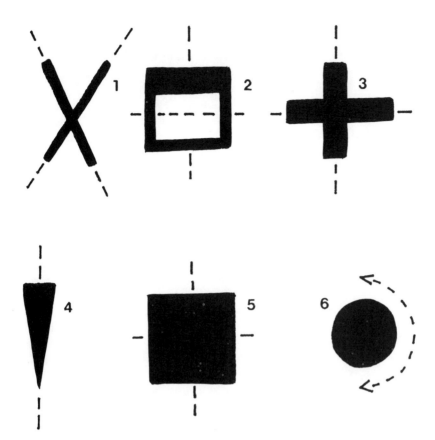

Fig. 8-1 Geometric shapes.

ends of these lines. You don't want points. Some practice in laying the brush against the glass will be necessary. The two lines should cross one another cleanly, without smudges. This can be accomplished while the underlying line is wet.

Shape 2 is an open square with one side thicker than the other three. Whether you paint this line first or last makes no difference. Again, bridge positions are indicated by the dotted lines; you will position the bridge four times, once for each line. The bridge will be held parallel and slightly away from the line being traced. When it comes to painting the one side that is thicker than the other two, increase the pressure on your brush to get the necessary width in one stroke.

Important: Get your lines to meet evenly; try not to run over. The object of these exercises is to have a complete little figuration using the brush, not to leave loose ends that you can "clean up" later. We will have a lot more to say about this particular philosophy when we discuss the use of stick-lighting. We want to stress at this point that these are brush exercises, and therefore the brush must be utilized to its full capacity. It should not be dependent on another tool to enhance its capabilities. Besides that, thinking you can "clean up" later is a very bad habit to get into.

Shape 3 is a cross made by outlining and filling in with brush strokes. The bridge will be positioned twice as shown. Again, take your time, but get the lines to cross while the bottom one is still wet. It doesn't matter which line you do first. Note the blunt ends of the lines. These are done using only the brush—no clean up with a stick. You should do the same. (Two well-placed strokes with a lettering brush will also suffice for this figure. No outlining is required.) It may take you a little practice to learn just how much pressure to apply and the most effective position of the brush to get these blunt ends. Once you get the feel of your brush, you will be delighted to find how much of the work it will do by itself. That's what tracing brushes are for. How to do the filling-in strokes properly is described below for shape 5.

Shape 4 is square-edged and carrot-like. No movement of the bridge is required. The purpose of this exercise is to practice brush pressure. In outlining, you will use more pressure against the glass at the wider end of the shape, splaying the bristles against the surface; less pressure is used at the narrow end where you will be dealing with the point of the brush. Don't rush this stroke. The tendency of some students, when dealing with a pointed line, is to sweep the brush off the glass. It isn't speed that gives you the shape, but control—and control requires a calculated, not a rushed timing. It will take some practice to learn this. You may also practice doing this figure the other way round, going from pointed to thick end. Your hand will get accommodated to going either way with comfort. Eventually you will consider this simply routine. Fill in the shape with one or two strokes (see instructions for shape 5).

In all these exercises, don't try to get each one perfect. The important thing is to acquire the proper finger motion. We've seen students spend a lot of time fiddling with "clean up" and outlining to get a "perfect" result. But this obviates the reason for practicing—which implies, by its very nature, the freedom to make errors.

Shape 5 is a solid square block and for some is the most difficult shape of this series. There are several ways to paint it. You will position the bridge four times as with shape 2. Outline with fairly thick lines; then fill in. When filling in, the idea is *not* to dab with the brush. In fact, it is best not to lift the brush at all when filling in. Get enough paint on it to fill in with one continuous stroke. Be careful when lifting your brush after filling in that you do not leave a heavy nipple of paint which may fry during the firing process. If your paint is of the proper consistency, it will assume the same thickness throughout the block. Don't rush the filling-in process, but don't take so long with it that your outline dries before you have completed the inside of the figure. Don't be careless—there is no reason for the filling-in process to overlap beyond the outline. Remember, though, not to get involved with cleaning up extraneous bits of paint. Anything beyond the borders stays there as part of the learning process.

Of the shapes so far discussed, this block is most likely to show a halftone, since it covers the most area. You may get your lines absolutely even and think you've gotten the square absolutely opaque. Then you hold it up to the light and see all sorts of wavy strokes going light and dark within it. It is discouraging. Be assured it happens to everyone. Do it again after mixing your paint more thoroughly. You may end up doing quite a number of these blocks, but eventually you will get an idea just what mix of paint will present the proper opacity, together with what kind of brush stroke will best apply it. Pinholes are another problem; as discussed earlier, these can be filled in.

Another way of painting this block is to outline and fill in at the same time. Use your thickest tracer for this so that the parallel lines you make will be wide enough to almost meet at the center. Whatever filling in is then required will be minimal. Of course, with larger squares this is not feasible, because the width of your tracing brushes will be unable to cover enough area per stroke to fill in the square. Basically, of course, this second technique is just a more rapid variation of the first.

Do not attempt to fill in without first providing yourself with an outline guide. We have seen students attempt to start from the center, fill in and try to make the outline part of the filling-in process. Inevitably this will lead to a sloppy end result with jagged edges of paint protruding beyond what should be a clean-cut border. This is usually done out of sheer laziness, the individual not wanting to take the trouble to move the bridge as required.

Shape 6 is a circular variant of shape 5. The dotted line here indicates that the bridge can be held in any position. This is a two stroke figure—essentially two C strokes with subsequent filling in between them. Do as much of these C curves as you can with your fingers, keeping the wrist motion to a minimum. Don't try to make the inside of the C curves perfect—they will end up as part of the filled-in circle anyway. It is not necessary to outline this figure in the sense of taking a thin brush, drawing the circular outline, then putting in the main body of paint in the center. This outline should be readily accomplished in two strokes of the tracer, without having to move the bridge from your chosen position. As with shape 5, you may find halftones when you hold it up to the light. Or you may find you can do the circle without halftones, whereas they continue to haunt you in the square block. This is because the square has more strokes and is angular; there are more beginnings and ends to lines. The strokes of the circle, being practically two continuous lines, will tend to flow together more readily with fewer chances of discrepancies in opacity.

All this series of exercises should be practiced alternately. Try not to stay with any one of these figures too long or to the exclusion of the others. If you keep doing the same one over and over you will start getting so inbred you may lose all sense of perspective and make more, not fewer, mistakes. When you feel you have this series down pretty well, go on to the next one. You can always come back to this one again.

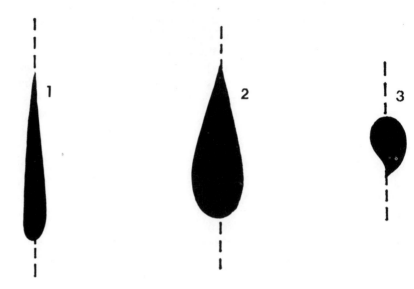

Fig. 8-2 Teardrops.

Exercise Two: The Teardrop

Figure 8-2 shows three examples of a basic teardrop shape we are going to expand on as we go along. There are many other possible teardrop shapes, and you can try any ones you want. Those illustrated here pretty well cover the extremes.

Teardrop 1 is a modification of a straight line. It varies from thin to thick in its length and has a point at its beginning and a rounded finale. This shape can be accomplished in a single stroke. Unlike shape 4 in exercise one, this figure is more easily drawn from thin to thick because of the rounded termination. You can try doing it the other way round if you like.

Teardrop 2 is a further modification of teardrop 1. This design will likely take two basic outlining strokes without any movement of the bridge. The stroke begins with little pressure to form the top point and continues with increasing pressure down either side, outlining and filling in as it goes, to approximately halfway round the circular bottom. The second stroke repeats the process on the other side to meet the prior paint line at the bottom. Whatever filling in is then required can be done. As usual, you will check your end result for halftones; as usual you will probably find them. It doesn't seem to matter how opaque you have gotten the previous shapes; every time you practice a new one, the halftones may return. Each exercise furnishes its own challenges—that's what keeps them interesting.

Teardrop 3 is a small, compact teardrop. It is really a small circle with a little tail, and it is the tail you might have trouble with. Try to make it follow ours as closely as you can. It only takes a little flick of the brush to accomplish this; the tail is meant to be a fillip, not a point of emphasis. This commalike figuration need not be outlined; it can be done as one continuous stroke, starting with the further curve in a backhand approach, carrying itself round, filling in as it goes, and ending with the little appendage. There should be a sense of flow, of spontaneity about it. The tail should not look forced as though it was added as an afterthought, nor should it be emphasized out of proportion to the main body.

We have not yet spoken of backhand strokes, but now it would be a good idea to practice developing them so you don't have to keep twisting your bridge around to get the lower part or the side part of a circle. We use the terms *forehand* and *backhand* to denote strokes going respectively counterclockwise and clockwise. C strokes are good for backhand attempts; practice them in different thicknesses next to each other for comparison. Do forehand and backhand C strokes, both facing you and facing away. You should not have to favor either one as you develop your tracing technique; you will need both forehand and backhand in tune as you get into more extensive tracing.

These exercises are further considerations of the teardrop design.

Number 1 is a basic straight line modification with a slight curve

*Exercise Three:
Teardrop
Modifications*

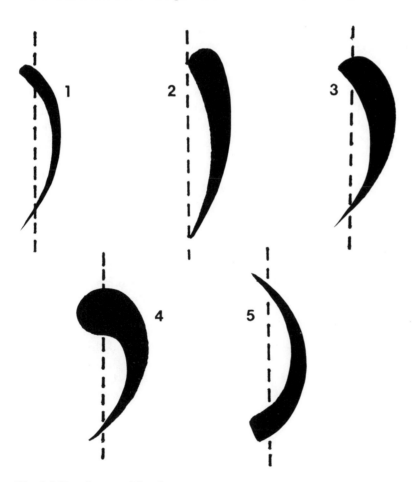

Fig. 8-3 Teardrop modifications.

going from thick to thin. The heavier end is somewhat blunted. This is one continuous sweep to the tail, releasing brush pressure as you go. It is imperative that your hand gets used to this motion before you go on to the rest of this series.

Number 2 has a rounded heavier portion, and the tail is somewhat more blunted than number 1. In tracing these shapes, try to make them look just like the ones shown. Don't assume that because differences are small, they don't matter. Each of these designs is meant to be a specific teaching experience, and the closer you follow them, the more of the tracing process you will learn.

Number 3 provides practice in holding the tracer at an angle, not straight up and down, and using more of the side of the brush to start. We are familiar with rounded, blunt, and square ends of lines. This design is sort of a cross between blunt and round, with a beaked top portion which the brush will make when held at the proper angle. Getting the brush to make the small point with the rounded head isn't so much the crux of the matter as is getting it to make the sweep from this new angle, following the shape given. However, the difficulty is more apparent than real. You will find, as usual, that your amiable tracer will do most of the work, provided you give it the proper guidance. It may take a little time to accommodate yourself to this new design, but you'll find with the hand sense you already have developed that it is easier to negotiate such variations in technique.

Number 4 shows a relationship to our friend, the comma. Here he is rather augmented, and you will probably have to take him in two strokes with a wide brush. You may want to put your newly acquired backhand into use. Start at the under portion of the head and swing round and down the tail. Then carry a small forehand stroke to complete the body and another stroke to fill in the head. If you want to try it, it is possible to do this design in one fell swoop with a wide brush, holding the brush hairs at the proper angle so as to expose a wide, flat area to the glass, and changing the angle to a more upright position as you curve round to the narrower sections. You should spend a lot of time practicing this design; there is a lot to be learned from it.

Number 5 has you making the curve the other way (as, of course, you can do with any of these curves by switching the position of your cartoon). In going from thin to thick after practicing just the opposite for a length of time, you may find your hand a bit obstinate at first. But it will shortly respond and the change in technique will only add to your control. As with the other exercises, once you have gotten through these, take a break and then come back and practice a few of these at a time before going on to the next series.

Exercise Four: The S Shape

These are the most advanced of the series of finger movements. Your success in accomplishing them will be based on what you have learned from the previous exercises. If you have done your homework properly, you will have found your strokes growing ever

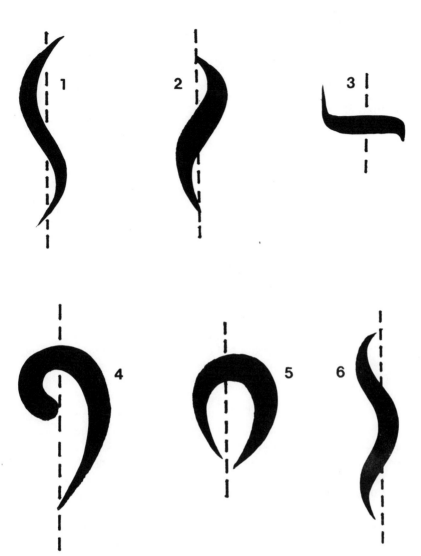

Fig. 8-4 S shapes.

more certain, beginning and ending where you want them to be, firm and opaque. If you are still unsure, if your lines are wavering and your starts and finishes smudged, relax. Go back to practicing the previous exercises and allow your hand sense to develop more. It *will* develop, almost instinctively—there is no question about that. The only individuals we have found who could not learn to trace were those who had thoroughly convinced themselves they never would. Some individuals are more adept at a skill than are others, but we are talking about a learned skill, not an artistic process, and if you want to do it badly enough, you will.

None of these examples call for any change in position of the bridge, and only minimum wrist motion is called for. These exercises are all combinations of pressure differentials, finger control and wrist excursions. When you have completed this final set you will be ready to utilize what you have learned in combination to make actual designs.

S shape 1 is similar to the S strokes we started with, but rather than the free-flowing, undisciplined lines you did at the very beginning, these are tightly controlled finger movements. In this first example we are using a combination of two C curves in different directions balanced along an imaginary equator. Utilize the extent of your fingers to their utmost as projected through the arch of the hand. Remember to keep the heel of your hand firm on the bridge. You should have no trouble getting the flow of this initial stroke. Don't hurry it; don't let the brush control your hand. At the same time, don't let it drag or your hand is liable to shake. Come down on the glass with your tracing brush like an airplane landing. That and a slightly increasing pressure will give you the gradual widening of the line from the point; taper it evenly to the tail by gradually releasing the pressure.

S shape 2 is a compressed pattern with less of a point at either end and more of a squat in-between area. You will have to land your brush on the glass and apply pressure a little more rapidly here than in S shape 1 since the point is much shorter. As you complete the stroke, you will have to take the weight up more abruptly for the same reason. It provides a good variation for alternating brush pressures.

S shape 3 is a horizontal line with two ends of unequal length going in opposite directions. This is a nice break from the previous routine of up and down strokes. Note the bridge position. You may have to stretch out from the bridge a little with the brush to reach the end of the line; that and coming down with the brush to make the initial thin stroke may take a little time to perfect, but it is well worth the effort. Your fingers should be able to bring the brush back toward the bridge, drawing it sideways, and add the final little downward turn after a few tries. It's all in the wrist and the arch of the hand, and these should be getting pretty flexible by now.

S shape 4 is almost a question mark. There is, however, no question about the amount of practice you may need to accomplish it. You should be eventually able to do it in one stroke, starting with a backhand turn and transforming the stroke via a small wrist movement into a forehand conclusion. All the way through are some interesting pressure gradients that we think will amuse you (depending on your mood).

S shape 5, an extreme carry over from S shape 4, is probably the most difficult figure in the series. You have to come down lightly with your brush to get that short, pointed beginning to the line in a backhand stroke, then carry it along in a tight curve with increasing pressure on the brush. This pressure begins to decrease as you approach the termination, still continuing that same tight curve as you take your brush up and off the glass to provide the final point.

S shape 6 shouldn't be too much trouble for you if you have managed the others already. It's a combination of three C curves, moving from thin to thick to thin, and provides good practice for pressure control and finger and wrist movement.

One final point about these basic tracing exercises: Don't attempt them all at once. Do a few at a time, then review them, then go back to freehand strokes, or just practice straight lines with the edge of your bridge as a guide. Then do a few more finger exercises. You may try to combine some of the newer finger exercises with some that you've done already. Invent your own shapes—but remember that you should first draw a cartoon if you are going off on your own. Just painting freehand is no discipline at all at this point. There are any number of combinations of the finger exercises we have presented. Challenge yourself to put them together in some creative pattern. It is all part of not getting bored with the practice, getting your fingers and wrist introduced to a motion that may be completely alien to them, giving yourself the satisfaction of seeing improvement occur from one practice tracing to the next.

Use these exercise cartoons in at least the four basic positions available by moving the cartoon. With each position you may find variations in approach which apply only to this basic position. The bridge positions in relation to the shape will, however, remain the same.

✥ CHAPTER 9

Tracing Borders, Drapery, and the Flower Vine

Now that you have your finger movements under control, we are going ahead to actual figurations that you are likely to run across in tracing projects. These may prove more interesting than the exercises you have practiced so far, inasmuch as each will provide you with a finished piece rather than just isolated shapes done for their own sake. We will discuss four separate projects in this chapter, each of which offers certain problems. With the experience you have gathered this far, you should be able to do them with a lot less difficulty than you might imagine. You may have some difficulty in that you are used to working with much smaller design elements in your finger movement practicing. We have purposely made these designs this size to involve more wrist and arm movement. We will start with the simplest, though at first glance it may look disconcertingly ornate. First trace these patterns onto paper and use the drawing for your cartoon under your glass.

Bordering: Open Design   The top square in figure 9-1 shows just what we mean by an open design border. This and many similar designs can be used for painted borders of windows or panels. There are three challenges in this design. First, there is the problem of drawing the square itself; second, that of tracing the design within. If you look at this design closely you'll see a lot of old friends, namely many of the finger movements from the preceding chapter. Some of them are out in plain view and others are rather disguised, but you should be able to relate to them quickly. The third challenge is the square within the square, which is a somewhat extended form of shape 5 in figure 8-1. So, all in all, there really isn't anything here you haven't already practiced. All we have done is rearrange the lines a bit and come up with a tracing "statement." Let's see how well you can do with it.

There are several places to start. You can trace the outside borders to begin with, or you can start with the internal design. Let us take the outside borders first. When you are tracing any sort of square or similar geometric figure, you will find that the right

108

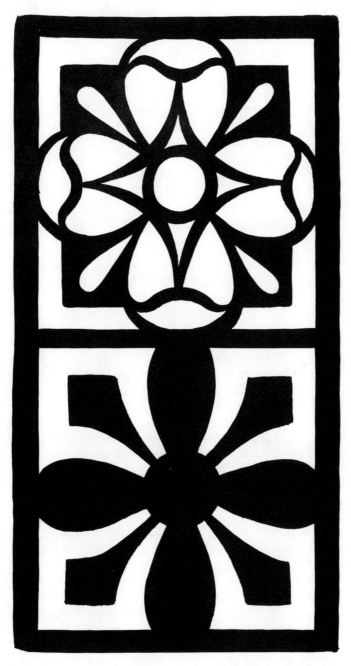

Fig. 9-1 Open border design (top) and closed border design (bottom). *Courtesy of American Glass Guild.*

Fig. 9-2 The tracing technique for the open border arrangement. What is wrong with this picture? You are right—the bridge is at right angles to the stroke rather than parallel to it. It may be fine as a hand rest, but it is no help to the tracing stroke.

angles where the borders meet can be somewhat of a problem. Don't be frustrated trying to get the lines as straight as possible as well as the paint to meet without forming a blob at the junction. Use the side of your bridge as a guide to make a straight line, and just pick up directly at the angles from one line to the next. You don't have to take each line into its neighbor—learn to stop your brush just at the point where the lines juxtapose. Try to meet the preceding line as neatly as possible; if you do go over, don't attempt to clean up your line with the light stick. Notice in figure 9-3 how the lines overshot the mark in the lower left corner. This kind of error is all right at first, though it shows more control of your brush to make the lines meet exactly.

In tracing the square many students have a tendency to move the brush either too quickly or too slowly. Too quickly and you will overshoot the juncture points; too slowly and the line may waver, even with the bridge as a guide. Keep practicing these borders until you get them just right. Develop a certain rhythm when tracing lines—even a straight line. It is one of the best of all work habits. Your rhythm may be slow at first, but try to maintain it for all shapes of lines. As you gain familiarity with the tracing procedure, your rhythm will begin to speed up, almost without your noticing, no matter what you are tracing.

Once you have the outside borders under control, turn your attention to the internal design. These are mostly finger movements and should pose few difficulties. (Notice how the student whose work is shown in figure 9-3 has practiced on the side a stroke he

Fig. 9-3 Student's work. Not bad overall, though the lower left corner will have to be cleaned up.

found difficult before including it into the general design. This is always a good idea.) The four large petals of the design each impinge to some extent on the inside surface of the borders you have just traced. It would behoove you, therefore, to start tracing these elements before the border dries. If your bordering lines are already dry, start with these petals anyway and, instead of penetrating the border lines with your stroke, just touch the curved lines to them, pick up your brush and continue the curve where it comes off the border. Good backhand strokes are required here.

With these petals traced, the rest of the design soon falls into place. The next element might well be the central circle which attaches all the inner lines. This will probably take two strokes, though you might like to try it in one. Incidentally, if you prefer two strokes, they don't have to be two evenly divided ones. You might start with a backhand and not be able to get all the way round. Pick up with your second stroke wherever the first one leaves off. From the inner circle progress to the four curved, pointed lines that border it, and from there to the S-shaped lines across the body of each petal.

The inner square, which is broken into four separate components, might now be painted. You might want to switch to a thinner tracer for outlining purposes. Outline not only the borders of these internal square pieces but the teardrop space within as well. You practiced teardrops in the finger movements as a painted positive statement; here we see them as a negative, clear glass effect.

With the outlining done (it can all be done at once, or each portion can be treated as a separate entity), you can fill in with your moderate or thick tracer as you see fit. Of course halftones and pinholes may be a problem but, again, using the techniques you have already developed, and understanding the reasons for each, should help you out of this difficulty readily enough. You should practice doing a number of these open designed squares completely before going on to the next exercise.

For purposes of contrast, we have placed both open and closed design squares in juxtaposition in figure 9-1. It is not necessary that you paint them that way, but you may if you wish. If you do, you will start the next square by extending the two sides of the one above and merely add the bottom line to complete the geometry.

This closed design exercise serves three purposes. First, it is an absolute haven for pinholes and halftones, and you will get plenty of practice in avoiding them. Second, it involves practice in outlining. Third, it will show you how to control your stroke, either when making the outline or when filling in so as not to get botched lines. Remember, there is to be no stick light clean-up. These are all brush exercises, and you will therefore want to do as good and complete a job as possible relying on the brush alone.

Let's take the possible difficulties. As far as halftones go, you already know what to do about those. This exercise contains the largest area so far that you have been asked to cover with opaque paint, so you may find you are not quite as good at avoiding halftones as you thought. Make sure your paint is of proper consistency and that you have adequately dipped and swirled your brush in the paint well to properly load it. For outlining, we suggest you use your heaviest tracer so as to get as broad a mark as you can, leaving less to fill in and, therefore, less likelihood of halftones developing. Try to fill in the remaining area with S-shaped strokes,

Fig. 9-4 Just to show you how nicely the designs can be accomplished by a beginning student, here is one large piece of window glass being employed for a three-design composition. The more you do, the better.

Fig. 9-5 Another student exercise demonstrating how many variations can be accomplished with just these simple designs once you put your mind to it.

and guard against leaving a nipple of paint when you remove the brush from the glass.

This kind of border element, with its silhouette effect, is quite dramatic—provided the edges of the design are clean. Nothing can so quickly ruin a bold statement as doubtful quirks round the periphery—in this case, irregular out-thrustings of paint from uncontrolled strokes. Outlining must be done with a sure hand. The most confident outlining, however, will be defeated by relaxation of control when it comes to filling in the body of the work. Believe it or not, this is where many students tend to go a little foul. Then, having overplyed the brush, they have to start using the stick light to reoutline and clean up—a bad habit to get into. Sloppiness or laziness will quickly become a dead end technically and creatively.

You can invent other bordering designs to trace, or find an infinite variety to copy from old windows. The more you do, the more refined your technique and sense of design will become. You will learn what works well and what does not, so far as these particular ornamental elements are concerned. In many instances, designs such as these are silkscreened onto glass to save repetitious labor. Our purpose here is not to produce a completed designed effect, nor to save time—but a practice session for tracing. You might make a project for yourself and take a large piece of glass and trace around it with alternating border designs. This has two purposes. First, it provides you with the necessary repetition to develop hand sensitivity, and second, it gives you a very dramatic, completed piece of work which you can judge creatively as well as technically.

Drapery: The Sleeve

How to make the folds in garments seems to be a major question in the minds of most beginning glass painters. Actually you can make them with many of the lines you have already been practicing. You can review them as you practice tracing figure 9-6. Here we have chosen a sleeve, a portion of a garment that has many folds and one that you can have some fun with by adding the missing hand. Note, first, the basic outline and how clean-cut and unwavering these lines are. Virtually all the movement in the piece is expressed through lines that are essentially straight in character. None of the individual lines should prove difficult for you to trace at this point; this exercise is as much to demonstrate a conglomerate effect as individual strokes.

Be aware that this sleeve is only one element of a particular type of drapery. It is an example and an exercise, and is not meant to be applied to all sorts of situations. For purposes of learning certain techniques, however, it will be invaluable to you. For instance, note the way the angles fall and complement one another to create a sense of flow.

Study other types of garments to understand how the trace lines are placed to get the initial, basic effect (see chapter 16). Look over the way cloaks fold into the body, the way lines are placed to indicate collars, the manner in which dresses are given a particular flow to flatter the human figure. All these examples contain trace line components evolving from your previous exercises. The execution of curls and folds of hair and drapery will become more obvious when studied as trace lines separate from their matt component.

That is not to say that drapery flow is entirely dependent on trace lines. In many finished works you will see that the tracing element has been reduced to a rather limited skeletal function from which the matt, the shadowing, takes over to fulfill the conception. However, the trace line is usually the formative element.

The sleeve tracing is one of three separate exercises that will be carried to completion, starting with tracing, through matting, highlighting, and ending with the staining process and the final firing.

The Vine

When you go to trace an object that has many differently shaped lines—large lines, small lines, thick and thin lines—it's probably a good idea to do the larger, longer lines first. However, this doesn't always hold true. While generally you might want to get the large strokes in before anything else and then tie the smaller strokes into them, there are instances where you might prefer to start with some of the more difficult lines and then work the rest of the figure in around those. With the difficult part out of the way, you can complete the rest with confidence and not risk spoiling what you have done by a weak termination of awkward strokes.

The vine (figure 9-7) is the most complex piece we have taken up so far. There are altogether twenty-one major strokes involved. A key to these strokes is furnished in figure 9-8. You may, of

Fig. 9-6 Drapery tracing: the sleeve.
Courtesy of American Glass Guild.

Fig. 9-7 Vine drawing.
*Courtesy of American
Glass Guild.*

Fig. 9-8 Key to suggested stroke sequence.

course, determine your own order of strokes but the order shown
in the key probably minimizes as much as possible any overlap-
ping of fresh lines onto dry areas.

Before starting the vine you should review at least two long tracing motions, the ones shown alongside the vine in figure 9-7. One
is a straight line with blunted ends; the second a long wavy line,
pointed at each end and varying in width throughout its length.
You will find tracing these lines very useful (don't do them freehand—use the lines as a cartoon). The finger and wrist movements we have been emphasizing may have made you overcon-
scious of developing a "small technique." You must retrieve some
of the initial spontaneity with which you started. You will also get
practice in moving your arm. Tracing several dozen of these lines
will help enlarge your hand sense and will add to the discrete
range of the fingers a spatial breadth of motion that is inherent in
tracing.

Once you feel limbered up, start tracing the vine, beginning with the top V (lines 1 and 2). You will probably find lines 6 and 7 the most difficult. To do them it is necessary to reach out from the bridge with the brush, pivoting on the heel of the hand, to the far starting points of these lines. Then you must make the transition towards the bridge and convert the stroke down along the bridge to terminate the line. It's a twisty sort of maneuver, but one you will run into fairly frequently, so it is best to get it down now. (You might want to review figures 7-26 through 7-32.)

As you can see, the leaves are the last lines we advise to be painted. The longer lines of the stems are first perfected—a series of Vs which, if you are not careful, will tend to make your brush run somewhat out of control. Try to follow these lines as exactly as possible and have them meet within the limits prescribed by the cartoon. Then tie in all the smaller strokes.

As you go along practicing the vine, you may begin to take a little poetic license with the cartoon. Each paint line may vary a trifle and needn't match the corresponding cartoon line exactly. While you may individualize some of the lines, don't do this to the extent that you are making a statement totally different than the cartoon. Tracing needn't be limited to a slavish copying, but the cartoon must always be acknowledged as a guide. Careful tracing is an exercise in discipline that helps establish control in use of the materials and a faithfulness to the guiding principle of the cartoon. However, you may now begin adding to your tracing technique a sense of your own personal style. Don't overdo it, though. In a studio situation where painter and cartoonist may be two different

Fig. 9-9 Tracing the vine. Note that the bridge is held from the bottom and is parallel to the tracing stroke. The brush is about 90° to the surface of the glass.

people, this could lead to emotional problems as well as technical. Your own style can be manifest in the way a line curves, the glide from a point to thickness, the taper, the manner in which your connecting lines meet. Tracing is not a mimicking of the cartoon; it is a translation of its guidelines into paint.

The vine should be traced as an exercise as often as you think necessary. Get it down pat. When you are done with it, you should be able to trace it practically with your eyes closed. It is a critical exercise, marking your own transition from neophyte to beginning tracer. Here is where you must pause and sum up everything that has gone so far. If you are unsure of yourself, don't be ashamed to admit it. Go back to the beginning and review everything we have discussed to this point. Redo the exercises involved. It is all training. The more you train, the better you will get. Tracing is a matter of practice, understanding certain rules and respecting both the potential and limitations of the medium. Once you learn that much, you are ready to devote this technique to creative processes that are far more satisfying than these training exercises, but technically grounded in them.

✥ CHAPTER 10

Tracing
the Head

With this project (figure 10-1) we leave the field of tracing exercises as such and are now going into a more creative endeavor. Don't be awed by the fact that you will be tracing a head. This project is composed of modifications of those same finger, wrist, and arm motions that have taken up so much of your time in the prior chapters. You should have little trouble at this stage in adapting your hand to this new combination of strokes.

We chose the head for several reasons. For one, almost every beginning tracer looks forward to producing a head. It represents a major step forward in development and skill. In fact, we found it was the challenge of doing a head that got many students interested in painting on glass. And, of course, almost every procedure and problem involved in tracing and matting is found in this particular subject. Because the challenges are so diffuse, the shaping of lines (to say nothing of matting choices) so subject to individual variation, the head provides an excellent summing up of all you have learned so far in the tracing field and a challenge to your abilities.

Where to Begin

Figures 10-2 and 10-3 give you an idea how this project can proceed. You may practice each element individually before putting them together. This will give you a good deal of confidence when actually tracing the head. If you have trouble with any particular group of elements, this is the time to overcome it.

When you go to do the head, we would start with the left eyebrow, eyelid, and eye (elements 1, 2, and 3). You can attempt these strokes with a thick tracer to get them all at once, or you can outline and fill in while the paint is still wet. There are three particular challenges here in the three sharp points—two in the eyebrow and one in the eye. Try to trace these as exactly as possible without changing brushes to do so. If you find that your thick brush blobs here, you are applying too much pressure. You can accomplish these points using the point of a thick tracer, though it may take a bit of practice to do so.

After you have filled in this area, hold it up to the light to check for halftones, and you'll find out immediately whether your trace is mixed properly. If you are getting halftones, scrape off the trace,

120

Fig. 10-1 The basic head for tracing and matting.
Courtesy of American Glass Guild.

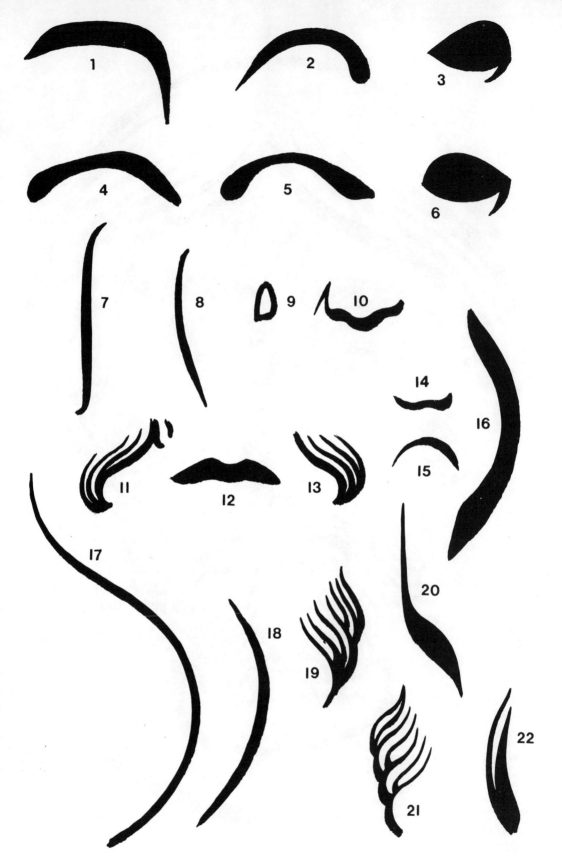

Fig. 10-2 Individual elements of the head.

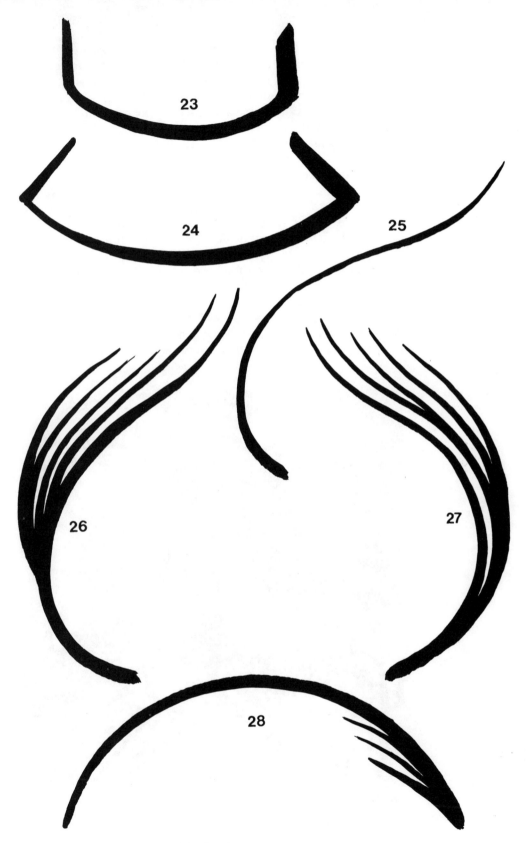

Fig. 10-3 Individual elements of the head.

remix your paint to a proper consistency, and try again. Better to find out now than later when you have the exercise completed.

Next trace the right brow, eyelid, and eye (elements 4, 5, and 6) and then down the right side of the nose (7 and 8). Next the nostril line and base of the nose and the right nostril (9 and 10); then the lines beneath the center of the nose and the left mustache (11), the lip and right mustache (12 and 13); then the underlip and chin (14 and 15).

We next turn our attention to the right forehead and cheek (16), followed by the forehead hairline(17) and the hairline between it and the cheek (18). Then down the right beard (19) to the center of the chin. The left cheek (20) is next, including the beard (21) on that side to the center line, followed by the hairline at the cheek (22). Next we would do the neck and then the collar (23 and 24), following this with the left forehead hairline (25). Finish with the remaining hair on the left and right (26 and 27) and do the dome of the head last (28).

The above procedure is only a suggestion and is subject to many variations. You might try following it the first time you do this head just to get the strokes under some sort of system, but you can

Fig. 10-4 Trace copy of a medieval window demonstrates how trace paint alone, with neither matt, stain, nor color, can provide an individual effect in a sketchlike approach.

Fig. 10-5 Another head traced with the same technique used for the head in figure 10-1. Note the amount of black trace paint used as a background.

easily develop your own methods which might be more convenient to you. Many students do very well beginning with the dome of the head, going from that point to the rather sweeping hair strokes, leading from those into the beard, to the neck and collar lines, and only then going into tracing the more specific features of the face. Still others prefer to concentrate on the features per se even before tracing the outline of the hair and beard. There is no one right way to do this exercise. Experience will soon teach you which is best for you.

One question that keeps coming up with this project is whether or not to use a separate small tracer for the beard. Since these are rather discrete lines and, of course, must not be blobbed together, we generally encourage changing brushes to accommodate this.

Fig. 10-6 A partially matted, totally unique version of the head in figure 10-1. *Courtesy of Jim Russell.*

However, these lines *can* be accomplished with the thickest tracer you own, utilizing the point of the brush with a very light pressure. Remember, in this exercise, these lines are strictly trace lines— we are not engaged in any sort of stick-lighting procedures. If your hairlines do not come out as brisk as you'd like, don't start using a stick to clean them up. Scrape them off and retrace them.

Difficulties with the Head

Some problems typically experienced by students tracing the head are discussed below.

1. Forgetting to move the bridge. Remember that the bridge is a

portable instrument. Get it into the position best suited for your comfort as long as you do not use it, consciously or unconsciously, as a hand rest. It should become second nature for you to maneuver the bridge to your hand, and vice versa. Don't try forcing your hand to fit an existing bridge position as a matter of convenience. The line that is traced under these circumstances may appear to be forced.

2. Dry spots. These are likely to occur in the eyebrows, eyes, and some of the thicker facial and hair lines. If you are outlining these areas, make sure your paint is flowing properly and flowing from the outlined areas into the center. If there is not enough vehicle in your paint, scrape off that portion of your trace that is "draggy" and add vehicle to your pile and redo those strokes.

Fig. 10-7 An etherealized version with stick-light on matt.

Fig. 10-8 Trace used to make a negative image.

Fig. 10-9 A student's portrayal of one of the authors, Dick Millard. *Courtesy of Jeffrey Pein. From a Tom Loya caricature.*

3. Too much vehicle. Too much vehicle will not only cause half-tones, but may cause the trace paint to run beyond the outlines of the cartoon. Particular areas of danger are the spaces between eyebrows and eyes. If this happens, do not attempt to use your stick to clean up, but remix your trace to a proper consistency, scrape off the mess you've made, and try again.

4. Mixing areas of dried and fresh paint. As noted previously, where this happens you may get frying when the piece is fired. Covering dried paint with wet usually occurs when students get so fascinated with a stroke that they continue on to succeeding strokes rather than going back to where it began. This is all right if you are tracing a thin stroke; with a thick one there can be a problem if another thick stroke imposes on it at one end. By the time you get back up there, your original stroke will have dried and the juncture between it and its neighbor could be a trouble zone.

When you are tracing any thick, continuous strokes, as on the left brow, cheekbone, and nose, be sure that you tie them together while each is still wet.

Variations   Once you have gotten adept at tracing the head, you can indulge your own creativity to a degree. Even without using matt or silver stain, a number of distinctly different heads can be developed from this one (see figures 10-6 and 10-7, for example). Succeeding chapters will show how trace lines can be made to provide different effects. Some of our students couldn't wait that long to express their

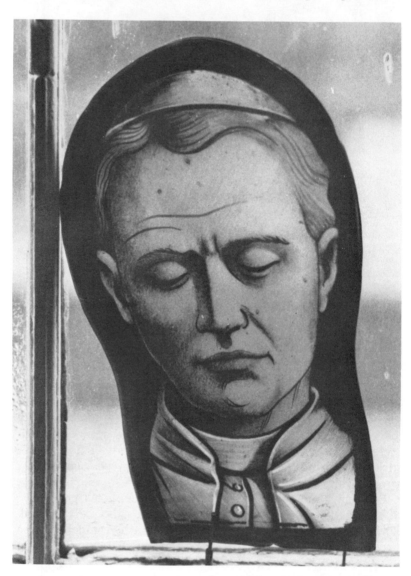

Fig. 10-10 This refined delineation of the head is accomplished in the tracing within the broad outlines provided by the cutline. The background is blacked in and the eye concentrates on the foreground. *Painted by Frank Kaufl. Courtesy of Richard Millard.*

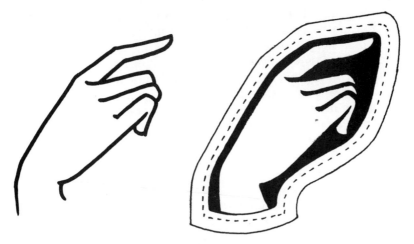

Fig. 10-11 An original drawing and cartoon, ready for translation to a cut piece of glass. Dotted line indicates the cutline for the glass.

individual personalities. Figures 10-4 through 10-10 show quite a variety of heads, all but two done with just trace.

The heads and figures shown in figures 10-4, 10-5, and 10-10 utilize a technique called perimeter tracing, in which the featured element is silhouetted against an opaque background. Other examples can be seen in figures 3-1 and 3-4. Perimeter tracing is a normal procedure in tracing. For instance, if you are tracing a hand, it is quite impossible to cut the glass to conform precisely to the drawing. The hand is first drawn, and a cartoon is made

Perimeter Tracing

Fig. 10-12 The glass blank is cut to approximate the shape of the element. The excess glass is blacked out with trace paint or matt, leaving the foreground in dazzling display.

(figure 10-11). The piece of glass that will contain the hand is cut as close to the general shape of the hand as is comfortable. The portion of the glass beyond the confines of the hand is blocked out with trace in as artistically defining a manner as possible (figure 10-12). The viewing eye skips over this blacked-out portion, concentrating upon foreground images. The opaque background does not get in the way of the totality of the picture any more than do the individual lead lines. Some students have a notion that in negative imagery, the glass is first covered with trace paint and the desired feature is then scratched away. This is not done in routine painting.

A good exercise would be to draw hands and feet in different positions, calculate different cuts of glass to contain and complement the flow of line, and then actually cut such shapes and trace in the parts of the body on them. Those portions of the glass outside the figuration would be "shadowed out" with trace. It is important, especially in heads, hands, feet, and designs of minute detail, to allow sufficient room between the outline of the feature and the glass perimeter so it will not be encroached upon by the lead. Once you start actually working with negative imagery it becomes a self-evident function.

Technical competence at tracing requires no art training whatsoever. All the same, tracing is not painting. The specifics we have provided are mostly mechanical. When we get to matting, you may find our instructions presuppose a certain amount of knowledge on your part, whether intuitive or more formally gained, as to painting in general. You may acquire this from actual training or just from observation. Our technical information, combined with your practice, will certainly enable you to become a tracer. To become a painter will require your contributing a certain aesthetic sense. We cannot teach that. However, by paying attention to highlighting and shadowing, to light and shade techniques as we describe them, by copying and practicing, through constant observation, you will begin to develop a sense of style based on what you have learned. Your use of it, how you refine it, the statements it enables you to make, will all bear a relationship to how well you paint and the type of painter you become. There are many excellent tracers. The number of really good glass painters is small.

PART THREE

Matting
and
Staining

✣ CHAPTER 11

Introduction
to Matting

Matt paint is not necessarily any different from trace paint—the two may be used interchangeably. While most matt paints tend to have finer particles than trace paint, the difference is not between matt paint and trace paint but between matting and tracing. Each process is employed for a different effect; each involves different techniques.

The tracing procedure implies linear detail using an opaque application of dark (not necessarily black) paint. The matting process is more satisfied by the use of a wash of paint for shadowing and highlighting. Matt is used to emphasize, enhance, subdue, modify, or vary the character of the glass. The matt may vary from piece to piece, or even within the same piece of glass. It should be used selectively and meaningfully rather than mechanically or excessively.

Matt comes in different colors, and its color would be chosen depending on the effect you want to produce. We frequently use an umber brown matt, or a bistre brown matt. There are also flesh reds, black/greens, gray/greens, and other matt colors available. Remember, though, that matt is used not so much to introduce color as to provide a translucent material that will give variations to the light transmission through the glass.

The different matt colors are more readily apparent on clear rather than on stained glass. Though many artists use colored matts on stained glass to get a "just-so" effect, it is debatable if in most instances the effect is not more in their minds. You are, of course, welcome to use whatever color matt you feel does best for your presentation. Matting, by complementing and emphasizing the quality of the glass over which it is placed, can provide effects from subtle to emphatic. If you happen to be using a very soft tone glass you might want to try a warmer color matt for the flesh to reflect its character the better. On the other hand, if you are doing a crucifixion scene or something equally dramatic, you may prefer to utilize a greenish matt to get that clangorous background to project more readily. Keep in mind that one depends basically on the color of the glass rather than on the color of the matt to make the essential statement. The matt is used to round it off.

On white or clear glass you might use a matt color that you

What Is Matt?

would find unacceptable on colored glass. Many students are confused by the number of matt colors available for purchase. Choice should depend on the "flavor" of the glass you are using, the scene involved, and the effect desired.

Mixing the Matt

Matt is mixed in the same manner as trace paint. (Hancock colors will have to be ground before mixing.) Water is the vehicle (for our purposes), and gum arabic is added at the discretion of the worker depending on whether a soft or a hard matt is desired. The softer you want the matt, the less gum you add. Many glass painters prefer a hard matt to a soft one (that is, one with rather more gum than less). Use of too hard a matt, however, will not allow you to achieve the subtle transitions between the dark and light shadowings that is the basis of good glass painting. Too hard a matt will also tend to chip and fragment as you go to remove lights from it, and it may fry when fired.

The softer the matt, the more easily you will be able to remove it from the glass with your highlight brushes and the cleaner the line you will get with the stick-light when you go to inscribe the matt. On the other hand, if the matt is too soft, it will wipe off the glass at its own discretion, not at yours. And if you trace over it later in its unfired state, you are liable to get a halation around the trace lines. This is due to there being more gum in the trace paint than in the matt. Consequently the matt will "suck up" this gum from around the trace line and cling to it in that area.

Experimentation is the best way to decide how much gum you like in your matt for a specific purpose. You can start by using about the same amount you know to employ for your trace paint and either decrease or increase from that level. Make some experimental blends and test the consistency with a highlight brush as you did the trace paint. Again, if there is a pulling or a chipping of the matt, it is much too hard. If it wipes off the glass too easily so that the character of the brush stroke is lost, then the matt is too soft and must be hardened accordingly.

Keep a separate palette for your matt. If you intend to be working in more than one color, maintain a separate palette for each color you use. As far as small brushes are concerned, you can use the same brushes for matt and trace paint as long as you are sticking to a water or vinegar matt. When and if you go to an oil matt (to provide different effects) you will have to keep those brushes separate.

Brushes

The brush that we have found best for applying matt to the glass is the 1½ inch series 18 (series A-1738) from Reusche. It puts the matt onto the glass rapidly and evenly, with clear-cut strokes. It's a rather expensive brush, but if you get the best to begin with, you will learn twice as much twice as fast and you won't later have to unlearn some of the bad habits inferior tools may saddle you with.

The most efficient brush to use in blending matt is, of course, the badger blender. In our opinion no really fine matting can be accomplished without it. This does not mean that blending matt is an exclusive province of this particular brush. Many other brushes can be employed to help blend matt, particularly in small areas where the wider badger would, in fact, prove awkward. However, over a wide area there is really nothing like the badger for accomplishing the job efficiently and getting the most precise result. Both the matting brush and the badger blender are discussed at greater length in chapter 5.

When involved in applying and blending matt to the proper degree, many students forget to clean the brush. It is important that you do clean it, however. This, too, is discussed in chapter 5. Just a reminder here—don't dust the brush against a sharp-cornered piece of wood or metal, as it will end up cutting your brush hairs. Many workers clean the brushes by spinning them in their hands. This not only throws the dirt and dust out of your blender (and into your face if you don't hold the brush upside down), it also flares the hairs—a characteristic that many painters like.

Using the Easel and Waxing Up

The matting process requires "waxing up" the pieces of glass to be painted on the easel. Rarely is matting done "down," that is, on the light table, except in the case of an individual piece of glass, small detail work (as in the case of Swiss Heraldic panels), diapering, and similar work that does not imply a sweep of matt across the glass. In this regard matting is just the opposite of tracing which is rarely done up on the easel.

Most hobbyists do not require the large, heavy easels that are used in studio situations, but if you are going to matt correctly, you should provide yourself with an easel of one type or another (see chapter 4). Just leaning a single piece of glass against a rest and placing a light behind it will not do. This is not only completely unprofessional, it is self-defeating. First of all, the matting procedure involves (usually) working on more than one piece of glass at a time. Secondly, blending your matt requires a stable set-up with no risk of the glass moving or falling over from the strokes of the brush. You will have enough to think about just learning to use the matt paint without worrying about the stability of some Rube Goldberg design.

An easel implies the use of wax to hold the glass to it. (If you haven't prepared your wax yet, see chapter 4). The wax is applied to the pieces of glass to be matted in a down position (the glass surface should be horizontal); a small dropperful of wax at each corner of each piece of glass is plenty. Provided you have the right mix of wax for the particular time of the year, you will have no trouble getting the glass to hold its proper position on the easel or removing it from the easel with minimum effort.

You don't want your wax to be too sticky or the piece of glass will slide down the easel; you don't want it to be too brittle as the piece of glass can then shake loose just from the vibrations of someone walking across the floor. It is a good idea to test your wax out before using it. Put it on a piece of glass as large as the largest piece you intend to use. The wax should hold this sample to the easel firmly. Next you should try chipping it off the easel to see how brittle or sticky it is. When you pry the piece of glass with your spatula the wax should immediately chip away and the piece of glass come cleanly off the easel. If it doesn't do this, that means the wax is too sticky and you must add resin. If the wax is not sticky enough, if the piece of glass doesn't hold, you must add more wax. Once you have your wax at the proper consistency, you should be able to wax up your glass pieces quickly with no loss of time, and remove them from the easel with equal facility.

Occasionally it is necessary to employ thumb wax, a type of wax which keeps glass or pieces of pattern on the easel but which doesn't harden. It is handy for special-purpose, temporary stick-ups, and a recipe for it is given in chapter 4.

Waxing up serves more of a purpose than simply holding your piece of glass to the easel. It gives you the proper perspective from

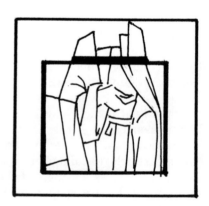

Fig. 11-1 The cartoon and connecting pieces. On the left is a cartoon showing the cutlines (the pieces of glass) with some hints as to where painting will occur. As seen on the right, when one section is waxed up on the easel, "connecting pieces" from the section previously painted are also waxed up as a guide for continuation of highlights.

which to view your work in progress, and allows you to apply and blend matt with the most efficient and effective strokes possible.

Waxing up also plays an important role when painting a large work over several sections, each of which contains many smaller pieces of glass. For example, figure 11-1 shows a cartoon with four large sections in the complete panel. As one completes the painting of a particular section and proceeds to the next, it's a good idea to wax up what are called "connection pieces." These are pieces of glass from the bottom of the section you have just done, since when painting sections of a window one generally starts at the top. It is necessary to align these with the top pieces of the next section so that you can properly continue highlights and matt consistency. Waxing up connection pieces is a necessary follow through from one painted section to the next when you don't have room on the easel to wax up all pieces of the window at one time. The first time you forget to do this, you'll find your highlights running from one section to the next are off. You'll never forget again.

Although this tool has been described earlier, we would like to go over a few points concerning it here. The mahl stick is not used like a bridge; it really is, basically, a hand rest. Glass painters do not use the mahl stick, as do sign painters or certain decorators, as

Using the Mahl Stick

Fig. 11-2 The mahl stick used as a basic hand rest, its padded end against the easel.

an integral part of the arm movement, but it should help, not hinder, your strokes. Generally the mahl stick comes into use anytime you are working on an easel at highlighting or texturing. When blending wide areas with the badger, you would have no use for the mahl stick. When you are matting and blending discrete areas, however, the mahl stick, used correctly, will prove invaluable in steadying your hand and guiding the brush.

The mahl stick is held in the nonworking hand across the body with the padded end resting on the glass (figure 11-2). The working hand utilizes it as a rest and/or a guide according to the activity involved (figures 11-3 and 11-4). There are no hard and fast rules as to the use of the stick; you will develop your own as you experiment with it. Like the bridge, you will not be able to think of certain aspects of painting without automatically reaching for the stick. You will routinely begin to position it at the point of maximum comfort for your stance and for the brush strokes you intend to produce.

The major difficulties experienced with mahl sticks are the following (usually due to homemade mahl sticks):

1. Mahl stick too long. This makes it awkward to use. It also makes it awkward for your neighbor, if you are working in a class, who has to keep dodging your lance. If you are working at home you may end up tripping or whacking your family as they come to admire your work. At the very least you will not be making it easy for yourself.

Fig. 11-3 Here the mahl stick supports the heel of the hand. Notice how it is further stabilized by one finger against the easel, permitting very controlled work to be done.

Fig. 11-4 The angle of the mahl stick can vary from parallel to the floor to almost right angles to it, depending on your comfort for the work in hand.

2. Mahl stick too short. You don't want to make it pencil length, either. The idea is to be able to rest your hand on it comfortably.

3. Using wood that is too springy. The best wood we have found is ½ inch dowel; some students use a piece of bamboo. You want the minimum of give to your stick unless you literally want to throw yourself into your work. There are painters who prefer a mahl stick that is somewhat springy, but we suggest a firm one.

4. Mahl stick too thick. Again, you don't want to get in your own way.

5. Mahl stick too bulky or too thin at its supportive end. You don't need to tie a whole bundle of rags to the end of the stick; you only want a reasonable padding to protect the glass and keep the stick from slipping. If you can feel the end of the stick through the padding, you don't have enough. Once you can't feel the stick through the padding, it probably is enough.

❧ CHAPTER 12

Applying and
Blending Matt

There are three processes involved in matting: applying it with the matting brush, distributing it with the blender, and the final blending. Begin your matting practice on a clear piece of glass. (We assume you have your matt mixed, brushes ready, and easel upright, as discussed in the previous chapter.) The initial idea is to get the matt onto the glass in as efficient a manner as possible, so that's where we'll start.

Applying the Matt

Matting up a piece of glass can appear to be a rather sloppy operation. There is a specific technique to it, all the same. For instance, your matt shouldn't start immediately to run down the glass. If it does this, chances are it is too watery (wipe it off, remix your matt, and start over). Nor should your matt leave bare spots on the glass, areas where it just doesn't seem to take. If it does this, your glass is probably dirty (figure 12-1). It's easy enough to get rid of this problem—simply rub the area over with your finger using some of the matt on your finger as an abrasive (figure 12-2). If your fingers are greasy, though, you will only compound the problem. If this is the case, a clean cloth, perhaps dipped in the matt, will quickly take care of the situation.

When applying matt with the matting brush you should have a

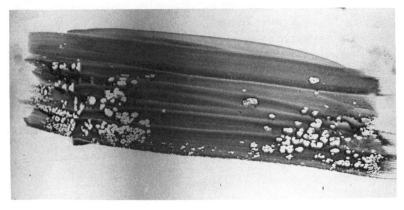

Fig. 12-1 Matt applied to glass with grease or grime on it will not take.
142

Fig. 12-2 One method of getting rid of dirt is to rub the matt over it with a finger. The abrasiveness of the matt will clean the glass.

set routine. It doesn't matter if you use only forehand strokes across the glass or use forehand and backhand, but it is probably best if your strokes run parallel to each other, as shown in figure 12-3. Some workers prefer to apply their matt straight up and down, but it is more likely to run down the path of the brush stroke. You can, if you want, run the matt every which way, but our suggestion is to do this only when small, discrete areas are involved. It is easier to blend the matt over large surfaces when it goes in one particular direction. (Your first stroke with the blender, then, will be at right angles to the applied strokes.) Your matting brush may tend to bend to one side as you apply matt with it. Just place the bristles in water and it will readily straighten out again.

Matt may be placed over fired trace or directly over clear glass. Whether you apply matt to clear glass or over the underlying trace,

Fig. 12-3 Matt is applied to the glass in parallel strokes with the matting brush.

the idea is to apply it smoothly so as to make the blending process that much easier. If you want to have certain areas darker or more opaque than others, you may apply more matt in these places to begin with, remembering that blending of these areas will lead to a certain dilution all the same. It is during the blending process that the values are finally consolidated.

In short, though there is not one particular method of applying matt, we suggest that you work out one for yourself so that you matt pretty much the same way each time, especially when matting an entire piece of glass.

Distributing and Blending the Matt

Once the matt is applied to the glass, you start the process of blending it; that is, spreading it evenly over that portion of the glass to which it is applicable. This can be a large or a small area, depending on the design of the painted areas.

When we talk about blending the matt evenly, we do not mean that every matt need be homogeneous. On the contrary. You may want certain shadowed elements to stand out, some other areas to be withdrawn. You may want some portions highlighted, others merely hinted at. But within these design bounds, to get the matt where you want it and end up with the proper texture, it must be worked. It must not only be evenly distributed, it must be, initially at least, literally pushed into position. This process, of getting the matt to those places where you wish it to be in the proper depth, is also implied when one speaks of blending the matt.

The technique we call blending is, in fact, a combination of two processes that can occur simultaneously, and to describe them separately could be misleading. For teaching purposes, however, it is necessary. The first process involves a distribution of the applied matt to the areas where you want it, in the depth you want it. Matt application is not an artistic process in itself; progress toward an imaginative effect begins with the distribution of this matt according to some plan. Only after this distribution concludes does the final homogenizing process, or actual blending of the matt, occur. Not having a grasp of this two-pronged activity is what confuses many students who assume that blending means simply spreading matt on glass, somewhat like filling in an outline with a crayon.

Distributing the matt must be done while the matt is still wet enough to respond. But matt must not be applied extra wet in an attempt to lengthen the distribution time, because then it will only run down the surface of the glass. On the other hand, we have found that many workers, especially beginners, work their matt in a medium or even semi-dry state because they've never gotten the concept that the initial stage of blending is really a distribution of matt to accommodate the basic values of light and shadow or flatness. So practice the technique of working the matt when wet, before it gets too dry to push around. A little experimenting will quickly tell you how wet your matt should be for ideal blending.

The same is true for how heavily you apply the matt to the glass with your matting brush. It may feel just right on the brush, but when you go to distribute it, you might find it too thick for proper mobility. If it's too thick, you will have to spend a much longer time distributing the values you want, and the longer it takes to distribute, the drier it gets, and the more difficult it becomes to work with. All of a sudden you find your blender removing the semi-dried matt.

Distributing matt that has been applied too thin is as bad as trying to work with matt which is applied too thick. Here the first stroke of the badger can all but wipe the matt off the glass. You may want this effect, which is fine; but if you do not, and it keeps happening, you'd best remix your matt and practice applying it heavier. You cannot catch up in a succeeding process what you skimped on in a prior one.

The homogenizing process (which most people think of as the blending process proper) occurs as the matt starts to dry, and it continues into the totally dry state. But at the beginning you literally have to shove the matt where you want it in order for it to end up in some rough approximation of the shading you desire. Then during blending proper, you can work the matt more finely within the range of values that you have initially established.

The basic blending stroke is rather precise. Many beginners tend to dab with the blender rather than stroke with it, to dust rather than propel. The idea is to follow a specific pattern with your motion. The figure 8 seems to be the most serviceable stroke. Let your wrist and arm relax. Let your arm come up, down and across, up, back and across. It may seem a bit artificial at first, but you will soon establish a rhythm.

The Basic Brush Stroke

Initial blending-distributing strokes should be at right angles to the applied matt (figures 12-4 and 12-5). After the matt is put on, start blending from a specific area, say at the top, and blend from left to right if your application stroke went originally up and down. Up and down application strokes are particularly useful if the matt is a little wetter than it should be, since it will be running downhill anyway and you can catch it by blending across.

The blender is not a duster. These original strokes are to place the matt, to put tides of matt where you want them. As soon as your matt is applied, go right into your figure 8 motion, stroking forehand and backhand, using both sides of the brush (figures 12-6 and 12-7). Don't be delicate; don't pretend you're painting wood. It doesn't take long to get the motion of the strokes right, and the rhythm is made easier by remembering to use both sides of the brush. We like to describe it as an airplane (the brush) touching down on the runway (the glass) and then taking off again. In other words, the motion is a curve which begins a certain distance from the glass, swoops down to touch the surface, travels along it for a distance, and then takes off again. You can practice your blending stroke even without matt on the glass. Take the

Fig. 12-4 The first stroke of the badger blender is at right angles to the strokes of the matting brush.

Fig. 12-5 Two strokes of the blender have pretty well erased the discrete lines of the original matt application.

Fig. 12-6 Further distributing of the matt, with the blender at right angles to its original strokes.

Fig. 12-7 Early results of figure 8 strokes done across the matt.

Fig. 12-8 As the figure 8 strokes continue, a homogenization of all these lines gradually occurs.

Fig. 12-9 The blending process continues with more strokes of the badger applied with increasingly less pressure.

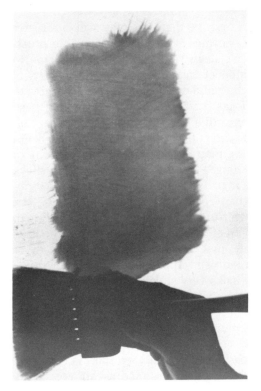

Fig. 12-10 The blended matt. Some faint brush strokes can still be seen. Further blending can erase these to a point where the matt will be as though feather polished, without the faintest brush stroke visible.

badger in hand and take the time to get the motion down. All this technique will enable you to proceed that much more efficiently to get the proper effects from the matt.

When you are landing your airplane (blender) on that runway (glass surface), it would behoove you not to touch down near the glass edge. This edge is often sharp, and if you keep dragging your blender into these edges you will find how rapidly it can begin to look dissipated. Occasionally hair will come out of your blender normally, but if you begin to notice obviously cut strands in your work, you had better look to your landing pattern. Blend *to* the edge of the glass, but not *from* the edge. The time to really beware is when you are matting up several pieces of glass and carrying your badger from one piece, over the edge, and to the next piece. Some of your brush bristles are going to drop down between the glass pieces and get dragged over the succeeding edge. Lighten your stroke somewhat as you approach the glass borders so that all the bristles can get free.

The major part of blending, the distributing of the matt, occurs in the initial stages. When you first stroke the matt, it will go in all directions, but as you continue the figure 8 motion, you will see the matt begin to even up under your brush. As you progress, gradually ease off the brush pressure; it becomes lighter, more delicate, feathery. At this point, you should be velvet-finishing the surface so as to leave no evidence of strokes. This final pressure is a far cry from the pushing of the matt that occurs in the first stage. (See figures 12-7 through 12-10.)

Cleaning the Brush

As you work your blender over the matt, the matt will get harder and drier, and as it dries, it becomes necessary to clean your brush more frequently. If you don't clean your blender, it will begin to leave a blotchy concentration of matt over the surface. This is because as you blend over drier and drier matt, the brush begins to pick some of it up. The bristles become stiff with paint, and these stiff bristles end up scoring rather than homogenizing what you have already blended. If you aren't paying attention, you will begin chipping away portions of the matt previously blended and have to end up redoing the whole thing. Furthermore, the matt that sticks to the bristles will dry the matt on the glass even faster as it absorbs water from it. This can become a vicious circle, and your matt may dry out even before you have it correctly distributed, much less blended. Last ditch efforts at trying to convince the matt to move are usually futile. So just wipe it all off and start again, or go over it with a wet matting brush (dipped in water or wet matt).

The blending technique looks very simple to someone who has never tried it. In reality it requires a lot of patience and a lot of practice to get the matt to do just what you have in mind before it dries. In this regard, it is much easier to work with an oil matt rather than a water matt, since oil stays moist so much longer than water. Despite its greater ease of workability, oil matt is best used over a water matt as a shadowing substance as an eye blend, cheekbone emphasizer, etc. So, no matter what you may hear about the more exotic matts, water matt still forms the basic substance on which all the rest build.

*Matting Discrete
Areas*

It is not necessary that matt be blended over an entire surface. Even a head need not be matted entirely. Many workers think of matt as a total blending, a homogenous surface. But matt is a tool that can be used to create all sorts of fascinating effects. You can matt a small portion of a head, arm, or leg, or a piece of drapery; leave the rest of the feature bare and use the matt to create a shadowing effect in another portion of the piece (figure 12-11).

Where only discrete portions of an underlying trace are to be matted, matt can be applied with just a touch of the matting brush and then immediately blended. When applying matt to individual areas such as a shadow under the eye or a darker area along the nose, this is one way it can be done—individual application and blending of matt, area by area, rather than applying all the matt at once.

In applying matt to discrete areas, you may not want or need to use the large badger blender. We tend to use small tinting brushes (a ½ inch Reusche series 16, for example) as blenders since we have found they allow much more control in these precise spots and push the matt more firmly into compact arrangements than does the wider badger (see figure 12-12). You may also find that a small brush gives you more control of halftone effects than does a wider brush that is meant, basically, to spread and blend the matt over larger surfaces.

Fig. 12-11 Matt has been applied and blended over one half of the face, with some experimental "stripe" matting on the other half. An example of the many imaginative effects that can be accomplished with matt.

Fig. 12-12 The matt is being pushed into the desired position with a blender (not a badger in this case) and it will then be immediately blended either with the same brush or a badger.

Fig. 12-13 Using the badger blender to blend a shadow into the brow and hairline. The other side of the head is left in shadow, completely matted.

Fig. 12-14 One half of the face shows total matting and blending. The other is matted only in specific areas and blended to form shadows. Highlights are now being taken out.

When you go to practice matting, we suggest you take the head previously traced (fire it first) and matt up the face and the hair. You might try matting up half the face and leaving the other half blank. In this manner, not only will you be able to get an idea of the extremes in effect between the matted and the unmatted sections, but once the extremes are established, you can continue the comparison by blending one side of the face with one technique and the other side with another. For example, blend in shadows under one eye, alongside one side of the nose. What is the immediate effect compared with the other side? Can you improve on what you have done when matting the other side? Give it a try. This comparison with one half the face and head to the other is an ever-fascinating exercise in composition. Which side looks better to you? Which is more natural, which more fantastic? Which side reads best from a distance?

Or take the chin, for example. Put some matt under the chin and blend it into a shadowed effect with one of your tinting brushes. Leave the head basically bare but continue to work touches of shadow into it. Now stand back and study the effect. You might do several heads varying this method, just shadowing portions of the face and leaving great streaks of light in angular motion playing over the features (figures 12-13 and 12-14).

So, you see, there are all sorts of ways of applying matt other

Fig. 12-15 When blending is complete, the blender can be used as a fan to get the vehicle to evaporate more readily.

than doing a complete wash. Of course when you blend in your matt in specific areas, it may spread to areas where it doesn't belong. You can remove this excess matt from those places either with your finger or with a highlight brush. Some students work very hard to keep their matt just within a specific area. Don't waste time on this. Create with splashes of matt. Put it on, blend it in, and then direct your attention to those discrete areas that you want matted. When you are involved with getting the basic shading values, you can't restrict your approach.

Another time when it is useful not to matt an entire area at once, but rather to apply and blend it in smaller individual areas is when matting a number of pieces of glass waxed into position. You may want to matt a few of them, blend these quickly, and, while the matt is still wet, apply fresh matt to the adjoining pieces and blend them. This way you avoid working with wet matt in one area with an entirely dry area of matt adjacent. If your blender accidentally brushes into a neighboring area of wet matt, it will not pick away the matt as would occur if the matt were dry. Keeping adjacent areas of matt moist will make the blending appear uniform throughout. Here is an instance where application and blending of matt are clearly all part of one flexible operation.

It's a good idea to trace out and fire several of the same head so as you practice matting this variable is constant. Then trace other heads—there are plenty of them available (see chapter 16 for examples)—and matt these. You will find the basic technique is the same. While each head is different, the matting technique, once you get it down, will work so in your favor that you will be astounded at what you can accomplish even with a head you've never seen before. It's all the same technique. So experiment, relax, have fun.

As we have indicated, most matting is done on the easel. Little matting is done down, that is flat on a light or work table. Not only is it inconvenient and inefficient to do several pieces of glass in this fashion, since it makes for awkward brush control, but it is also almost impossible to get the proper perspective on your work when you are using the matt to create shadows and highlights.

All the same, if you go into some studios you may see individuals matting down, or even holding the piece in their hand. Chances are they are using the matt merely as a blended background without any further character of its own. Such matting is usually reserved for small, unprepossessing portions of the work which only need some matt spread on them to meld them into the overall picture. So if you want to matt only a small piece of glass, using the matt just to modify the texture and transparancy with no relationship to any other piece of glass, for simple convenience it could be matted down. Apply your matt with the matting brush and blend, holding the piece in your hand.

One particular problem generally occurs when beginners matt down in this fashion. The heat from your fingers supporting the glass from below will lift away the matt in those areas (figure 12-16) and when you finish blending you will have three or four clear spots in the glass where your fingers supported it. It doesn't take

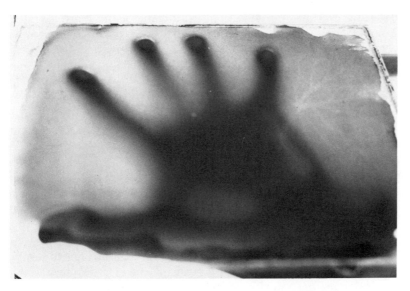

Fig. 12-16 Matting down means not using an easel. One of the quickest ways is to hold the piece of glass in one hand, matt it with the other. Soon, however, heat from the fingers begins to lift the matt away from the glass. Here you can see where the contact points at each finger and at the palm are beginning to affect the matt.

long for your finger heat to penetrate right through the glass. Usually it occurs after the matt has been blended and you are holding it waiting for the matt to dry. You may not even notice the spots until you put the piece down (figure 12-17).

The way to get round this is to work rather quickly. Apply the matt, blend it in rapidly, and put the glass down. It is probably best to try to support the glass from below by the edges; if the piece is too big for this, you might support one edge against your chest. Granted, this can get a little awkward, but if the piece is that big you would probably be better off matting it up on an easel anyway or down on a *clean* table.

Matting on the Reverse Side

Either side of the glass may be used to matt on, and many artists matt on both sides to achieve a desired effect. Matting on the reverse is often done to strengthen the values without taking the time for multiple firing of the piece. It makes no difference whether you fire matt up (toward the heat) or matt down (toward the shelf), although there are individual workers who believe there is a difference. There is no problem firing a piece of glass matted on both sides if it is laid down with care.

One caution: if you intend to matt on the reverse side of a piece of glass, remember that the paint may be exposed to the elements, and over a period of many years, the glass paint can deteriorate. Of course, if the piece is meant for strictly interior use, there is no problem.

Multiple Matting

For certain effects of light and shadow, succeeding coats of matt may be applied, either on the front or the back side of the glass. Matting overlays are often done with some of the more exotic oil and alcohol vehicles. However, much the same effect can be captured by the use of multiple water mattings.

The purpose of multiple matting, literally laying one coat of matt on top of another, is to achieve a range of value that cannot be accomplished with a single matting. Shading, density, tone differentials, and other modeling effects can sometimes be only partly derived through a single wash of matt. Yet, when you go to augment it, you can end up ruining the whole thing because of the impermanence of this unfired matt base. Obviously, it would be better to fire your original notion before attempting to augment it in any way. Once fired, you have an unshifting base on which to define further densities and tone values. In this manner, applying water matt after water matt and utilizing low (tack) firings (1050°F to 1100°F), you can build up your matt to achieve whatever densities you desire. You must be very careful not to fire too high, as this can fry the paint and shrink the piece of glass so that it no longer fits into its allotted space in the cartoon. Once this piece of bad luck and poor planning occurs, you have little recourse but to go back to the beginning.

Commercial studios do not like to spend the time required by multiple firing of one water matt on top of another. They would

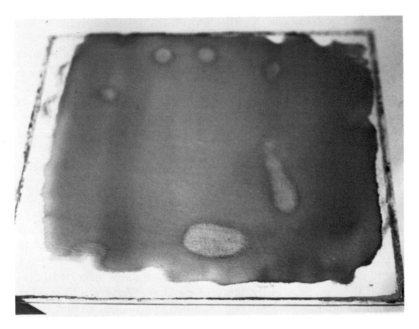

Fig. 12-17 With the glass placed on a table one can readily see what has happened to the matt.

much rather fire the kiln fewer times, getting more of the job done with each firing. This requires multiple matting with vehicles that will not interfere with each other in the unfired state. Such matts are dissolved in "resist" vehicles, that is, diluting agents that will not mix one with the other. An alcohol or an oil matt will not mix with water, so it may be used on top of an unfired water matt. A three-layered matt of water, alcohol, and then oil alleviates the necessity for any intermediate firing between their placement. Indeed you can build up these layers to almost any extent, so long as the different vehicles do not mix. Each layer can back up the one below, adding texture, density and differences in light without the loss of time involved in any intermediate firings. Stunning effects have been achieved this way.

As you may imagine, there is little margin for error in multiple matting of unfired paints. Specific techniques are involved in the various applications, and, in fact, an entire area of study, specific to this kind of painting, awaits the would-be practitioner. The application of some of these matts requires a trained, light touch, special stippling brushes, an advanced sense of humor, and considerable experience. Don't even attempt it until you have acquired a sure grasp of water matting technique. Otherwise frustration and waste, both of time and of money, are sure to follow. We mention these more exotic matts only to acquaint you with their existence and to specify that 90 percent of the effects achieved with these exotic applications can be accomplished by building up water matts discriminately and utilizing multiple firings.

When using multiple matting and firings, it is not mandatory to stay with the same color matt. You may, for instance, want to add a touch of green to a basic flesh tone. There's no reason why you cannot do this, keeping in mind that the final color will be a blend of the two layers of matt. We have found that our preference is either umber brown, which is a light flesh tone matt, or bistre brown. We also like the Hancock red for a nice flesh tint. Often we use the umber brown as an under matt, and after firing that in, use either a flesh red or the bistre brown over it to emphasize shadows, values, and details.

Once you fire in the base matt you can experiment with the overlay. If the second color doesn't achieve the effect you have in mind, all you need to do is wash it away and try again with a different color, or else fire it and make further modification with more matts and firings. It doesn't matter how many times you fire your piece of glass provided you do not overfire it. If you do happen to overfire, don't throw away the piece of painted glass. We have found that such "errors" can still make attractive window hangings if the design is sufficiently interesting. Well-done fragments can be fascinating. No one but you need know it was all part of the learning process.

✑ CHAPTER 13

Highlighting

Highlighting, also called "taking out the lights," is a technique of matt removal that provides areas of greater light and transparency in a work than the original matting would allow. Although it is a painting technique, it is not one you *have* to use. Matting can be an end in itself without a single highlight being added if this is the kind of effect you want. In most cases, however, the matting process leads to the logical next step—taking out the lights. This is a very potent technique of using transmitted light that can be, literally, dazzling. The secret is knowing just where to place the highlights, how intense to make the individual lights, and whether to grade them in intensity or have them in abrupt transition.

Essentially highlighting is the reverse of drawing. In drawing you generally place shadows in; in highlighting we take matt out. The method of this taking out is an art form in itself. Matt can be removed partially or completely; highlights can be double or tripled matted, depending on the effect you want to produce; matt can be removed abruptly to provide one effect or gradually to provide another. This original matt is removed with highlight brushes that are specific to the type of highlight required.

The Nature of Highlighting

If you intend to place highlights, your matt should be laid down with this in mind. It should have enough intensity to allow both primary and secondary highlights to go into it readily. Highlighting, therefore, is something that is planned from the start, even before the piece is matted. It is not something that is thrown in afterwards to try to jazz up a bland conception, though too often it is used in this fashion.

For a matt to take highlights well it should be resistant and not too soft; that is it must have enough gum in it. Many painters seem to place matt in so spongy a fashion that it doesn't have any sort of character or depth, and the highlights have little effect as a result. Glass painting is generally meant to be seen from a distance, so if what you do on the glass vanishes from across the room, what you have done is fairly useless as a statement. This is why it's important to practice matting before getting into highlighting—to understand that matt must have a character of its own, that it is not simply used to "fill in" open spaces.

Glass painting requires dark and light in extremes in order to be really effective, and it requires variation, as well, between these extremes. The matt, trace, and the highlighting procedure contribute

157

to all this. When any of these techniques are slighted or poorly used, the consequence is a work that is bland, unassuming, and generally forgettable. Examples are shown in figures 13-1 and 13-2. In these one can distinguish very few highlights. One reason is that the matting is poorly done. The artist has used a short bristle brush as well as a very hard matt, and there are sudden stops and starts in the brush strokes. This imparts not a transition of matt but a chipping of it. The faces, as a result of poor technique, have all the character of a bowl of porridge. The shadows in the faces are simply lines and shapes that have been stuck on rather than developed naturally from the physiognomy of the face itself.

A word to keep in mind when highlighting is *chiaroscuro,* meaning a juxtaposition of light and shadow. The ability to appropriately combine light and shadow is something that you can begin to un-

Fig. 13-1 Lack of variation in light and dark gives this face a bland appearance. The hair is well done.

Fig. 13-2 Here, neither face nor hair is well done. The face has little or no character. The hair and features are sketchy.

derstand by looking at a lot of paintings and studying certain ones that appeal to you in this regard very closely. These do not necessarily have to be glass paintings but can be oils and watercolors as well. Our own preference is the Italian Renaissance masters, but you can get the idea from whichever school you admire—the technique is universal.

Primary highlights are the areas of greatest matt removal and the point from which, in most cases, modeling in stained glass commences. The transition from intense light to shade is accomplished through the taking out of secondary lights, areas in which only some of the matt is removed. Shadowed areas are portions where the matt is left untouched.

Primary and Secondary Highlights

Figure 13-3 shows the basic head with what we consider to be the primary highlights. These are small areas of intense light, the positions and shapes of which are based on light over the viewer's left shoulder and the anatomy of this particular face and head. Remember that this lighting is only valid for this view of this model. The light can vary in direction as well as intensity; the head can be turned in any direction. But for this specific view, the primary lights shown would be the sources of brightest illumination; and they would be taken out completely to the bare glass.

Figure 13-4 shows the secondary lights. Note that these are actually pools of half light, spreading out from the focus of the primary highlights. Compare their shapes to the primary lights. The secondary lights tend to radiate, and are larger than the primary lights, but far less intense. They help add dimension to the piece.

Secondary highlights are usually taken out with a different brush than are the primary ones, and, as will be seen shortly, the process is one of erosion rather than abrupt removal.

Highlight Brushes

Highlight (or scrub) brushes can be any cheap bristle brushes that you can acquire from an artist friend or pick up on sale at an art supply store. Don't pay a great deal of money for these, since you will be cutting them down to particular shapes. Almost no highlight brush is used in its original configuration, unless it has developed an interesting one from use. You will want an entire series of shapes from which to choose (see figures 13-5 and 13-6), because each brush will create a different effect in the matt. The shaping of these brushes depends on the particular use to which

Fig. 13-3 Primary head highlights.

Fig. 13-4 Secondary head highlights.

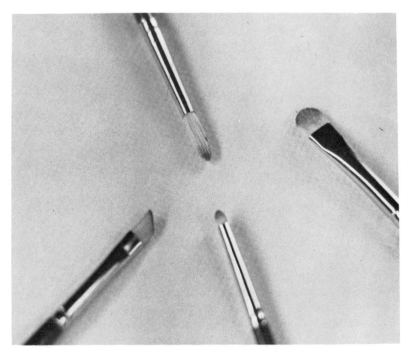

Fig. 13-5 A few of the many possible shapes of highlight brushes.

Fig. 13-6 A comparison of brush effects. The two brushes on the right are highlight brushes shaped from the two brushes on the left. Note the difference in their effect on the matt.

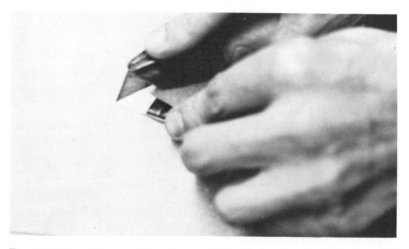

Fig. 13-7 The bristles of the future highlight brush are trimmed to an approximation of the desired shape with a sharp knife or scissors.

each is going to be put, but whatever shape you want to cut, the procedure is the same.

To make a highlight brush you first cut the shape with either a razor blade, sharp knife, or scissors, leaving the length a little more than you want to allow for wear during further refining of the shape (figures 13-7 and 13-8). Place a flat piece of metal on an electric burner. Make sure the bottom of the metal is indeed flat or you will impart whatever roundness or irregularity it has to your brush when you go to sear it. A clean aluminum pie plate or paint

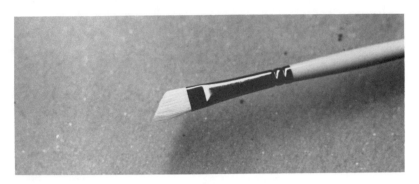

Fig. 13-8 The brush cut to shape.

can lid will serve. Heat this piece of metal to a temperature where the bristles will respond, and shape the bristles against this hot metal (figure 13-9). You will see the bristles turn brown from the heat. Keep checking the shape, taking the brush on and off the plate; turn it in your hand and reapply it to the plate to remove any irregularities.

As it gets close to the shape you have in mind, remove it from the heat and run it over a fine sandpaper (figures 13-10 and 13-11). This will get rid of the brown areas as well as refine the shape of the brush. You will probably have to alternate between the searing plate and the sandpaper to get the brush just right (figure 13-12). It is only necessary to rub the brush lightly along the sandpaper to mold the bristles; if you continue to rub briskly and at length, you will eventually be left with only the brush handle.

The shape of your highlight brush will continue to garner subtle refinements from the abrasiveness of the matt, which, in the course of time, will wear your brush to the point where it is no

Fig. 13-9 The highlight brush is further shaped on a hot plate. Make sure to hold the brush at the proper angle, and check the shape often.

Fig. 13-10 Remove the brush from the hot plate when it has a closer approximation to the rounded angle you desire, even though it looks a bit ragged from the effects of the searing.

Fig. 13-11 Rub the bristles over fine sand paper to get the final modifications.

Fig. 13-12 The finished highlight brush, smooth in all angles and rounded at the bottom so individual bristles will drag. This type of bias brush is very useful.

longer usable. We recommend, therefore, that when you make highlight brushes, you make two of each shape. By using them alternately, they will last twice as long before you have to cut, shape, and break in a new one. We do a lot of work with bias brushes, finding them very versatile because a number of shapes are incorporated in them. You have the front, either side as a right and a left stroke, as well as the back.

In highlight brushes, the shorter the bristle, the more matt will be removed. The longer and more flexible the bristle, the less matt will be removed per stroke, and you will be getting more of a half-tone effect, a transitional zone from the highlight into the matted, shadowed areas. Thus the longer the bristle, the more subtlety it will provide. Comparatively long bristle brushes shown in figure 13-13 are mostly flat in nature to allow for this stroking effect. Since they take out less matt per stroke, they can be worked longer over the matt than a brush that scoops a lot of matt at one time. Such a brush is also necessary, and one that you might find very effective is bullet shaped. This one has had its bristles shaped from a longer, rounded character to a little bullet-nose (second from lower right in figure 13-13). A certain rigidity in the bristles allows it to be used almost as a small eraser. Using such a bullet-shaped brush will allow you to push into an area forcefully, removing matt all at one stroke along the width of the brush. Such a bullet shaped brush is essential in highlighting. It can be used to remove a large or a small amount of matt, and for thick or thin lines.

Our own favorite shapes include the bullet, a longer, more wispy cylindrical brush, at least two flat brushes of varying length, and a moderate and an extreme bias brush (the latter takes some practice to use efficiently). You can take it from there. If you are using old brushes to make your highlight brushes, be sure you clean all the old paint and dirt out of the heel of the brush as well as out of the bristles. If you neglect to really scrub out this portion of the brush, you will get this dirt into the matt.

Highlighting Technique

Highlights are not simply taken out as holes in the matt and left that way. Some of them, at least, should be softened to get more dimension into the face or physical feature. Creating a highlight is done by first removing matt entirely with the appropriate brush and then blending an area of the remaining matt to create a semi-transparent or translucent effect around the primary light. The process of modifying the matt to accommodate the primary lights within its surface is what is meant by secondary lights. To modify the matt around the primary light, you can use a straight or a criss-crossed stroke, or you can stipple or otherwise texture it. The usual (and probably most effective method) is to blend it, for which you will use some of your specific highlight brushes. When blending, think of the matt as though it were a skin over the glass. You want to brush away only the very thinnest layers at a time.

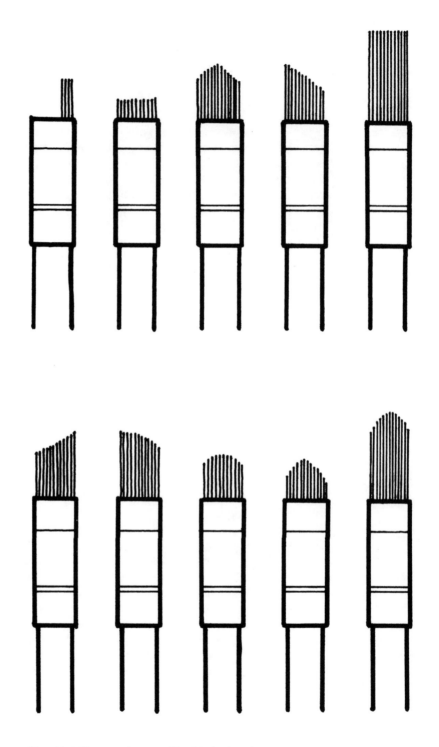

Fig. 13-3 Various shapes of highlight brushes.

This means going over and over the matt with the brush until you achieve just the effect you want.

Highlighting is not an easy procedure, and you may ruin what you are hoping to achieve. Don't be dismayed. Practicing highlighting is not nearly so tedious as practicing your original trace stroke. In highlighting you are working with a product that needs only the finishing touches to make it complete.

Highlighting should be done up on the easel, using the mahl stick to support and steady your hand as you work. Before matting up a head and attempting to place the highlights, just matt up a piece of glass and learn how to use your brushes to best advantage. Acquaint yourself with what each shape will do best and how much pressure is required to achieve various effects. Use wrist as well as finger movements. Try a gradual, blending removal of some highlights as well as abrupt removal. In short, get familiar with the procedure as a whole before turning to detailed highlighting. When you think you know your brushes well, then go on to practice highlighting on the head.

Once you get to the head, practice matting and taking out highlights as indicated in figures 13-3 and 13-4. A good place to start is with the highlight in the forehead. Be careful not to overdo it here or you will end up taking out too large an area of the matt. Some students keep trying to even up this circular highlight, and in their enthusiasm remove more and more matt until there is too much removed for the primary highlight and not enough left for the transition, secondary light. In highlighting, taking out a little bit is often more than enough. The examples of highlighting in this chapter show removing the lights from just one surface of the glass, though you can take out highlights on the other side as well. This is done by applying matt on the reverse side and taking out the primary (smaller) highlights on the back and removing the transitional secondary lights from the front. Some feel this makes the head look fuller when seen straight on in full frontal light.

Taking out the lights should make it look as though light is striking the piece from without. The classic type of lighting comes from over the left shoulder of the artist and falls on the painting, creating shadows and highlights from that direction. This is as true of glass painting as it is of painting on canvas. When removing highlights, do not go contrary to your presumed light source. Don't become confused by the fact that the actual light source is behind the glass. The source of the light is transferred through technique.

Keep in mind that the more intensity there is between the highlight and the surrounding matt, the more effectively the face will read from a distance. A certain blandness will be apparent if there are no highlights or if the lights are too large and poorly developed. From a distance you should be able to see a distinct play between the light and dark portions of your finished work. That is what makes the piece read.

Knowing where to place highlights is dependent on your skills in observation and visualization of the normal contours of the face and other parts of the body, as well as of direction of light source. Any portrait, painted or photographed, will give you varied highlights based on these conditions.

Figures 13-14 through 13-17 show a face being worked freehand on a matted and blended piece of glass. It is a spontaneous sketch, yet shows a clearly defined development. This is a good exercise in the placement of anatomical highlights and shows what can be accomplished by a simple play of light and shadow. Figure 13-18 shows a similar example. This type of exercise is important to clear the cobwebs from your mind when you are trying too hard to attain a strict sense of design. Such a good-natured, free-flowing approach can familiarize one with the materials and placement of lights more readily sometimes than more formal methods. You will be surprised what you can create out of matt.

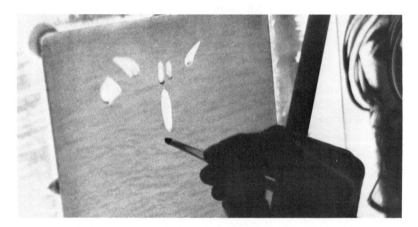

Fig. 13-14 A face is worked freehand through the use of highlights alone. Here the primary highlights are being removed.

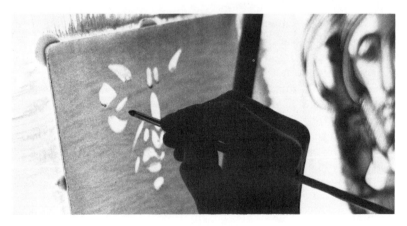

Fig. 13-15 The side of the face is highlighted to look as if it is reflecting light coming from over the artist's left shoulder.

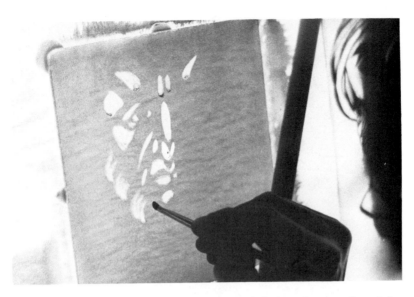

Fig. 13-16 The transition between light and dark is being softened by halftone removal, done either with a longer-bristled brush, or by fainter pressure with the bullet-shaped brush.

Fig. 13-17 The final head, getting a bit of a hairdo. Negative and positive lighting, strickly due to the matt, is the entire source of strength.

The face shown in figures 13-19 through 13-21 is somewhat differently organized. It began with a few trace lines on the reverse side of the glass under the area of blended matt. The trace lines are the foundation for building the face with highlights. As you can see, the trace lines are a great help in defining the features and strengthening the portrait.

It is important to remember that in highlighting you are, in es-

Fig. 13-18 Another type of head from matt alone, using the same basic technique as before but a little more ornate.

sence, painting with light. One of the purposes of highlighting is to make the head, or whatever portion of the body is being presented, look credible within the conceived style of the work. That is to say, the highlights need not be realistic. In fact, they can be decidedly unrealistic, provided they are logical within the span of the presentation. For example, just because a figure is drawn with one foot in an impossible anatomical position, doesn't mean the drawing is wrong. One need not take it literally. A foot can be purposely placed to show motion or to make a statement. Such a drawing is accurate creatively if not anatomically. The same idea should be kept in mind with highlighting. It doesn't matter if you deviate from a realistic approach (which after all is only one way of looking at things), provided that what comes out in the glass is a positive statement true to its own prerequisites. Highlighting enhances the idea behind the painting, makes light itself an emphasis.

Fig. 13-19 Trace lines on the reverse side are the foundation for creating this face through highlights. Here we see the beginning of characterization by the highlighting of cheek, forehead, and bridge of the nose. The beard is also being formed.

Fig. 13-20 The face begins to stand out more strongly with definition brought about by the sharpened highlights.

Fig. 13-21 The other side of the face was highlighted without back-up trace lines. A comparison of the two sides of the face shows unquestionably that the trace lines strengthen and provide focus to the physiognomy.

Fig. 13-22 Several examples of the same head, each with a different set of highlights. Study and compare them. Which looks best to you and why? Which shows the most effectiveness, which the least?

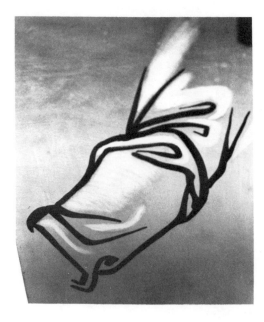

Fig. 13-23 The sleeve used previously as a tracing exercise may now be matted up and used for a highlighting endeavor.

Figure 13-22 shows several faces, traced approximately alike, each showing a different set of highlight elements. Look how different each head appears. The highlights tell them apart, providing separate characters, special outlooks. These few modeling resolutions only hint at the great variety of possibilities inherent in the medium. Even further modifications can be promoted by differences in matting and blending techniques such as texturing. The possibilities are vast.

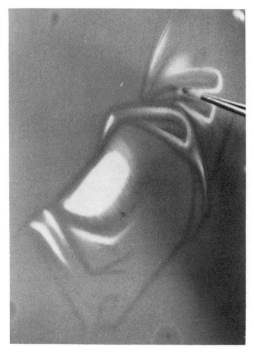

Fig. 13-24 Another attempt at drapery highlighting.

Fig. 13-25 Carrying the sleeve to its logical conclusion, a robe and figure are added by student Jim Russell. It just goes to show one never knows where these exercises are going to end.

In these heads, none of the highlights have been placed in an arbitrary manner. Each obeys the two rules we have set down: each is anatomical and each reflects light coming over the worker's left shoulder. The differences are stylistic. These depend on the widths of the lights, the distance from one another, the differences in line, the amount of shadow, the intensity of the light . . . and, of course, such creativity as the worker can impose. That factor, the others presumed, becomes the most potent of all.

The highlighting of drapery must be done with the same attention to anatomical structure and its effect on folds and flow of fabric, and to light source and its effect on shadows and highlights. The sleeve tracing exercise can be fired and used to practice on. Two resolutions of this exercise are shown in figures 13-23 and 13-24. You can also test your painting skill by completing the rest of the robe and adding a human figure (figure 13-25).

Highlighting through Multiple Matting

Another method of attaining primary and secondary highlights that can give even more depth occurs with multiple matting. For us this means multiple firings, since we are limiting our approach to water matt. It is done in a manner opposite to that just described. Here you can take out the secondary highlights first.

What you would do is to break down the head into its areas of light intensity, from the smallest but most intense (primary) to secondary and tertiary lights. You can carry this almost as far as you wish, depending on the amount of transitional zones you want to build in. Having determined how much matt you want to leave untouched, you now take out completely all the widest (tertiary) lights right down to the bare glass. Now you fire the piece and, once it has cooled, rematt. Now you take out the next zone of lights. This area will still be wide, but not so wide as the previous one. Fire once again. And so you keep repeating the process, each time adding matt and taking out less, each time edging closer to that central primary light, which may be left bare, or given a faint coating of matt so that it will blend in, depending on the effect you want. It will still be in contrast to the light radiating from it, which gets fainter and fainter as you go toward the shadow. Figures 13-26 through 13-29 show a painted demonstration, a "bull's eye," just to give you an idea what these transitional zones can look like. This type of highlighting is not difficult to do. It takes patience and successive firings, but is most effective.

Double matting highlights is a thoroughly fascinating technique. We have only indicated the many variations possible which, no doubt, you will want to experiment with yourself and build upon. The process need not go as we have described it; you can start with the primary highlight and go from there, just the reverse of the above process. You would then keep adding matt, and re-

Fig. 13-26 Multiple matting begins with a large highlight, shown here as a clear circle within the matt.

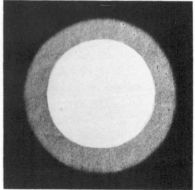

Fig. 13-27 A second wash of matt is applied after firing, and the center portion is removed again. The primary highlight in the center now has a rim of secondary, darker highlight around it.

 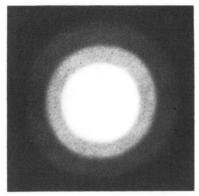

Fig. 13-28 The same process re-peated. The central highlight now radiates through the two secondary highlights into the darker matt.

Fig. 13-29 The same process re-peated. The central, primary high-light is now small and intense and radiates through successively darker layers of matt to the darkest portion.

moving more rather than less. We prefer the method we have de-scribed above because we find we can work out the highlights bet-ter that way. Double matting takes time; multiple matting takes a lot more time and a lot more kiln work, but the end results you can achieve with this technique can be truly outstanding. Should you get into oil matting, you will find you can utilize the basic tech-nique of multiple matting to provide a very strong impact, with these other vehicles over the base water matt, and accomplish it with, perhaps, only one firing. In the meantime you should prac-tice with your water matt. Most painters work only with water matt—and get just about the same results as with the more exotic alcohols and oils. There is practically no limit to the effects you can get with your painting when you begin to put all the elements so far discussed into operation.

✍ CHAPTER 14

Inscriptions

Inscribing lettering and lettered devices on glass windows is an old technique which has never really dropped out of fashion. Used mostly in the past as dedicatory provisos separate from the main body of the glass, with the newer crop of artists on the scene today, inscriptions are being worked more closely into the actual design. Their use as discrete titular endeavors continues, however, unabated.

Positive inscribing is just like tracing, only your lines are used to create letters, and it could just as well have been covered in the section on trace painting. Negative inscribing requires the laying down and blending of an opaque, even layer of trace or matt, into which the letters are inscribed. Inscribing is normally done down on a table or light table, not up on an easel.

Positive Inscribing

Positive inscribing implies placing trace paint over glass following an underlying cartoon. In this it is exactly like tracing. The bridge and tracing brushes are employed to follow the guidelines as with any other form of tracing exercise. More is demanded of the tracer in inscribing letters than in any other form of tracing since the preciseness of the script allows for little deviation from the cartoon. A good traced inscription of this nature should come out looking as though it had been done by a printing press, albeit with a certain spontaneity, to be sure. An example of positive inscribing, Hebrew lettering done by Dorothy Maddy, can be seen in the color section.

We recommend using letters as guides for tracing exercises. Alphabets are available in art supply stores, and lettering books can be found in many libraries and bookstores. Start with fairly large letters if you feel unsure of your hand, and work your way down to smaller and smaller sizes, always being critical of any wavering of the brush strokes.

It's not enough, though, just to practice separate letters. You should trace complete words and groups of words to become familiar with the spacing between letters and to train your eye to recognize any deviation from the underlying base line. Don't stick to just English lettering. Foreign alphabets furnish some interesting twists and turns that will prove a challenge to your tracing ability. It is also easier to criticize what you have done when the basic shape of the letter is unfamiliar to you. The eye tends to try to "even up" what is familiar. Hebrew, Greek, and Russian are alphabets that are readily available and will have some interesting sur-

178

prises for you when you get involved trying to trace specific words. Once you master these letters fairly well, English letters should be a snap.

Negative inscribing is actually a form of stick-lighting in which you take out, rather than add, paint (figure 14-1). Before work on the actual inscription begins, you should carefully plan the lettering on paper, showing the exact arrangement, size, and spacing of the letters.

One begins a negative inscription by matting the piece of glass with a black tracing paint. Use plenty of paint, applying it with the matting brush as thick as you can to get the maximum of opacity. Blend the paint with the badger nice and even (figure 14-2).

It is important to mix the paint properly so it will flow well. In this type of inscribing you will probably be covering a wide area of glass and you don't want clumps of paint blotching the surface. It might be a good idea to mix a drop of glycerin into the paint to get it to flow as evenly as possible. Because of the large amount of paint and vehicle, you may find that drying takes longer than usual. You can use your blender as a fan to increase evaporation of the vehicle, but make sure your blender is clean when you do this. Any dirt landing in the matt may not show up until after the piece is fired.

Once you have applied and blended your matt and are sure that it is dry, you are ready for the next step. Take a very soft white marking pencil (use a white china marking pencil or a Mongol white pencil) and make very faint guidelines for the inscription on the black matt (figure 14-3). The first pair of the guidelines should provide for the height of the letters. Use your third or fourth

Fig. 14-1 An ornate negative inscription, shown with a diapered adjunct. Both negative inscribing and diapering work pretty much by the same rules. Both are essentially ornamental; either can be a positive or negative process. *Courtesy of Arduth Grey.*

Fig. 14-2 A trace matt is applied and blended over a piece of glass.

Fig. 14-3 Guidelines are lightly drawn with a white marking pencil.

fingers as a guide against the glass edge (make sure it isn't sharp!) and draw a thin line parallel to the edge of the glass down its length. Draw another closer to the edge, paralleling the first. Your letters should fit between these two lines. Also mark the center of the inscription area (figure 14-4, top).

Now refer to your drawn lettering of the inscription. Obviously you cannot use it as a cartoon because of the opacity of the matt, but you can plan indirectly from this "blueprint." The first thing to do is to determine the center of the inscription. This will correspond to the center you have marked on the matt. To figure out the center of each line of lettering, simply measure each line in your "blueprint" and divide the length in half. Once you have established the center letter (or space), you will work forward and backward from this point. Before you approach your matted piece

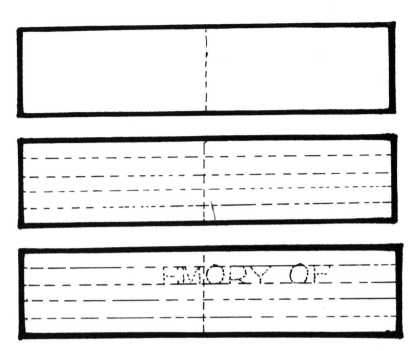

Fig. 14-4 Top: Parallel lines on the matt mark the height of the letters. The center is also indicated. Bottom: The letters are drawn in dotted lines with the marking pencil, starting from the center first one way, then the other. The letters are then inscribed with the stick-light.

of glass, however, lay a piece of paper over the bottom portion of the matted area so that the palm of your hand won't smudge it.

Now, start with the middle letter and indicate it with a dotted line made with your marking pencil on the surface of the matt. Do not push so hard with your pencil that the point goes through the matt. Once this letter is outlined as you wish it to appear, do the letters to either side of it in the same manner (figure 14-4, bottom). If there is a space to one side of this middle letter, remember to leave room for it. Once you have all your letters outlined in this fashion, step back and make sure that (1) the letters are as even as you can get them, (2) the spaces between words are approximately the same, and (3) you have spelled all the words correctly. It is embarrassing to provide a commemorative window with the name to be honored plus or minus some of its original letters. The problem with doing inscriptions, especially one after another, is that it is easy to grow careless. As a safety measure you would be wise to have someone proofread what you have done before going on to the next step.

The next step is to take your stylus (stick-light) and, following the dotted guidelines you have provided yourself, take out the matt (figure 14-5). A satisfactory stylus is essential in obtaining crisp borders for your letters. It should be of wood that is neither too hard nor too soft. If the wood is too hard, it will slide too readily on the glass surface and be difficult to control; if too soft the point will quickly blunt as you work and begin to pull away irregular furrows of the matt. Chapter 15 tells how to make one.

It is also probably best, from the standpoint of eye strain, not to use the light table when doing negative inscribing. You really don't need all that light from below coming up into your eyes. Instead, use a clean piece of white paper under your glass. This will usually enable you to see how the thing is coming out without having the spectre of the inscription in front of you for the rest of the day. However, the glass has to be pretty clear for you to do this. If the glass you are inscribing is darker than a tint, you may well have to use the light table in order to see what you are doing.

Doing inscriptions of this nature can be a tedious business, so it is totally justified to sit. Make yourself as comfortable as possible so that your work will not appear to be strained in any way— neither hurried nor cramped from your own lack of ease. Provide yourself with a stool high enough to be on top of your work, look- ing down, though not so high that you have to reach down to it.

Negative inscriptions can be taken out freehand. It isn't difficult to do this once you've trained your hand. It is simply a matter of practice; there are no tricks to it. If you feel more secure with a guide, you can utilize a straightedge to help. You must be careful of course to keep your straightedge from moving around and displacing the matt. Even in its unfired state, however, the matt will tend to cling to the glass quite strongly so you needn't be too timid.

On pointed letters such as A, V, N, W, you might allow their points to peak above and below the guidelines. This is particularly allowable when there is no serif involved. (Serifs are small bars or strokes at the ends of letters.) With curved letters such as O and U, the top and bottom of the O and bottom curve of the U can overhang the guideline at the point where it meets it. This pre-

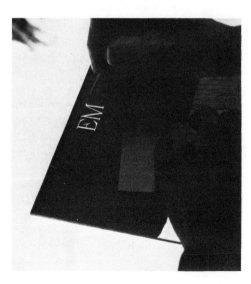

Fig. 14-5 After the spacing is calculated and the let- ters faintly marked in white, the inscribing pro- cess begins. Note the paper beneath the work- ing hand to keep the matt from smudging.

Fig. 14-6 After the last word is completed, the front portion of the phrase is attempted. Working from the front to the center is not always a good idea, as can be seen in figure 14-7.

vents the letters involved from appearing too short when compared with other letters in the word. All serifs should go directly on the line. When placing portions of a letter above or below the guidelines, it isn't necessary to exaggerate. Just the tip going above or below the line is enough to provide the proper effect.

Be prepared to make mistakes (figures 14-6 and 14-7). Unfortunately, most of these mistakes—taking out too much of a line or misjudging the distance between words—are not reversible. You can't add paint to make them up. If you can live with the error and want to take a chance that your client will, too, then fire up the piece and see what happens. Obviously firing isn't going to correct anything, though one maintains a wistful hope that it may. Any gross mistake clearly indicates starting the project over from the beginning, with a total reapplication of matt. What you might do is to matt up several pieces of glass at the start when it is as easy to do several as one. Then if you ruin one, you have another right at

Fig. 14-7 It is easy to make mistakes in inscriptions.

hand to take its place. Knowing you have a back-up piece can be a big help in keeping your standards and your spirits up.

Many painters make a big thing of inscriptions—how difficult they are to do, how much art is involved, how hard on the eyes. They can, indeed, be hard on the eyes, especially if you are turning out a lot of them all at once. However, as a creative process, inscriptions tend to become rather mechanical after the first fifty or so, and you will probably be surprised at how rapidly you pick up the technique and how good your inscriptions will look. All you have to remember is to follow the routine we've laid down. Remember, also, that you should have a fairly hard matt for inscribing into. The matt must not be so hard that it chips away, but firm enough to hold the stylus point within it with no mushiness of the lines. It must also, of course, be firm enough to lay a triangle or straight edge on it should you wish to do so. The cleaner the borders of the letters are, the more effective and jewel-like the lettering will appear from a distance.

✿ CHAPTER 15

Special
Techniques

We can't hope to cover all the variety of techniques brought to the field of glass painting by painters we have known and admired; nor would this be a necessarily rational goal because many techniques we have marveled at were effective only in the hands of their originators. However, a number of special techniques are certainly worth incorporating into your repertoire, and in this chapter we would like to describe some of those we think are most important.

No, we aren't getting into infant's wear. The word *diaper* also means "an all over pattern consisting of one or more small repeated units of design or geometric figures connecting with one another or growing out of one another with a continuous flowing or straight line pattern." Diapering, as applied to stained glass painting, involves a repetitive sort of design, almost an embroidery. Looking at some of the old diapers one is reminded curiously of wallpaper selections. The figurations can be spare or ornate, depending on how this would fit in with other portions of the window. There are two methods of diapering glass. In positive diapering, the pattern is painted onto the glass like tracing (see figure 15-1). In negative diapering, the paint is taken out of the matt as a form of inscribing (figure 15-2). Our discussion of diapering will be limited to this latter technique, since positive diapering can be accomplished by following tracing techniques already described.

Diapering, then, means removing matt from glass in an ornamental manner—à la engraving. A sort of stencil effect is provided. Diapering can be done along the borders of the glass or within the substance of the painting as ornamentation to clothing or·to form part of a predetermined background pattern. The work is done with a stylus (figure 15-3). Diapering, if done correctly, will read from a distance like delicate tracery on the glass or point up glistening areas of light within the body of the window or panel. Like many other techniques, diapering should be used sparingly so that it doesn't end up over-powering the piece it is only supposed to ornament.

A good diapering stylus almost has to be handmade. It is a very personal instrument. You can make one readily enough from a ¼-

Diapering

185

Fig. 15-1 Portions of traced and matted ornamental designs.

Fig. 15-2 Positive and negative diapering examples.

Fig. 15-3 Negative diapering is done with a stylus.

inch hardwood dowel about the length of a pencil. One end of this can be sharpened to a point in a pencil sharpener. The other end should be ground to a smooth chisel edge using a grindstone or sandpaper and emery cloth. Don't make the chisel edge perfectly straight, but let it round off somewhat (see figure 15-5). You will find more use for this chisel edge than for the point, though many students erroneously believe the point is the basic working end. The chisel edge is used to outline the form you are going to inscribe, and the point is used just to take out the finer areas. There are many wonderful effects you can accomplish with the chisel edge. You can get everything from a very narrow slice to a wide slash depending on how you put the chisel edge to the glass.

Diapering is fun, and most people catch onto the technique quite rapidly. Figure 15-4 has several examples for you to experiment with. As with inscribing, rest your hand on a piece of paper placed over the matt so you don't smudge it. Other than that, there really are no rules to diapering. Be free and off-hand with it, especially when you are practicing. Don't worry about putting too much diapering into your beginning panels—in fact you should do this purposely just to see how far you can carry the technique before it loses its effect. If you want to achieve a regular, repeated effect, make sure you dot out with white marking pencil the general plan of the lines you intend to inscribe, similar to the technique used for planning inscriptions. You can use your chisel edge to make the basic designs in the matt, and the pointed edge to take out very fine lines. One warning: though diapering is essentially a simple technique, it shouldn't be rushed through on that basis. It can look very sloppy if the lines are unkempt, if the inscriptions are uneven. Don't think that because it is a design, not lettering, that you can get away with slovenly work. Because diapering is so show-offy a technique, your mistakes will stand out all the more. Clean lines, a good thickness of matt and an evenness of the in-

Fig. 15-4 Examples for diapering practice.

scription—as well as an imaginative design—will help your diapering stand up as well as stand out.

Stick-Lighting

Although diapering is a form of stick-lighting, we use stick-lighting to refer specifically to taking out small portions of matt to create small, individual effects rather than an overall pattern. For instance, you can take straight line highlights out of a face with a stick when all you want is a thin line to show. Sometimes we stick-light on one side of a trace line to emphasize some feature of it. Stick-lighting can be employed as part of a traced and matted pattern to furnish yet another effect. And stick-lighting can be used to break a heavy trace line into some design that will be pleasing to the eye.

As with negative inscribing and diapering, stick-lighting is done with a stylus or stick-light (figure 15-5). Make them yourself out of ¼-inch wooden dowels, wood skewers, or good quality chopsticks. If a stylus is too hard, it will slide on the glass, and if it is too soft it will be spongy, so do some experimenting with different kinds of woods. Ash and maple are good woods. Pine is too soft. Metal points such as a needle or small nail embedded into a stick may also be used for fine detail work.

The stick-light is a very versatile device, and as such is often overused. One thing the stick should not be used for is as a crutch to clean up sloppy work. The stylus may be used to clean up small errors, or to make a line look a little better, but it should be used sparingly and not as an excuse to do careless tracing. None of the careless trace lines that you have "cleaned up" will look much better with all the marks of scraping along their edges. But even if they did, all this extra work is simply wasting time. Why not do it correctly in the first place?

Stick-lighting doesn't require the use of the bridge. As with inscriptions, you can cover the matt with a piece of paper to avoid smudging it, or keep your hand high so it is off the matt entirely.

Stick-lighting can be a very dramatic technique; as with diapering, don't overuse it.

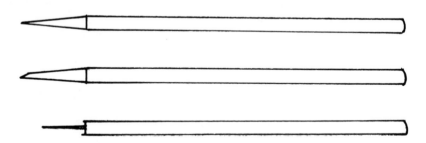

Fig. 15-5 Several examples of stick-lights for inscribing matt. Top: Pointed stick, sharpened in a pencil sharpener and sanded. Middle: chisel edge, cut and sanded smooth. Bottom: needle imbedded into the stick. One stick can also be made with two differently shaped ends.

Because a blended, homogenized matted surface tends to have a certain blandness, all sorts of devices have been utilized to give it "character." Interesting patterns can be accomplished in any one of a thousand different ways, in either wet matt or dry. We have already discussed stippling with the blender or a stipple brush (see chapter 5 and figures 15-6 and 15-7). Other methods abound. Anything from rubbing it with your palm to twisting crumpled newspaper over the matted glass seems to be fair play.

Try experimenting with varying forms of texture. We can't describe all the effects possible, but one effect we particularly are fond of is achieved by spritzing small splashes of water on the matt. This is done with the glass down on the table, and you must be careful to drop only a small amount of water at a time. Spritzing is done with a short bristle brush for a fine texture and a longer bristle brush for larger droplets.

The problem with texturing is the same problem that goes with other dramatic effects such as stick-lighting. It can be readily overused. Our suggestion is to underemploy rather than overemploy this particular technique. Your guidepost should be the nature and character of the glass itself. If your texturing is unique, ornamental, and provocative, it may still be too much for the glass. Texturing, like other forms of painting on glass, must be subservient to the medium. Otherwise you might as well be painting on

Fig. 15-6 Stippling in wet matt with the blender (left), a long-haired pig bristle stippler (center), and a short-haired stippler (right).

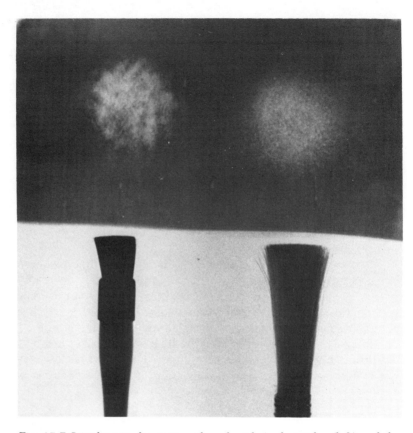

Fig. 15-7 Stippling in dry matt with a short-haired stippler (left) and the pig bristle stippler (right).

canvas. Texturing should appear to be called for by the subject matter, not just put in for the sake of the effect alone.

Quilling and Needling

Quilling and needling are both specialized forms of stick-lighting. The stylus used for stick-lighting is a more versatile instrument than either the quill or the needle, especially if made the way we suggest with that little chisel edge, and it is generally employed before either the needle or the quill is brought into play.

Needling is used to get a very fine texture into the matt. The needle is used to scrape, not to dot the matt as some students assume. By scraping with the point, very delicate lines can be imparted to the matt which read exceedingly well from a distance (figure 15-8). Needling provides a texture almost impossible to achieve with anything else. However you can also go a little crazy with this technique, aiming for effects next door to microscopic which may be appreciated by another glass painter but which will be blatantly overlooked by everyone else. It depends how fine you want to get to satisfy your artistic urges.

The needle you use is best placed in some sort of handle. If you

Fig. 15-8 The needle is used to scrape delicate lines in the matt.

have a doctor friend you may be able to get some needles that are already fixed within a glass barrel. If not, you can make a handle for your needle with a piece of narrow dowel. Make a tiny hole in the dowel with something other than the needle, and then stick the needle in with a little glue to help it hold. A handle provides greater mobility to the hand when you are using the needle; it also places the needle a little distance away from the hand so you are not working in your own shadow or getting in your own way. Needling can provide you with almost lace-like discrete effects as final touches; again it takes practice and patience to learn how to get the proper results with this tool.

Quilling is another form of stick-lighting, using a goose quill to produce fine effects in the matt. With a *good* quill you can get effects approaching that of a needle, or remove matt in a manner similar to a good stylus. So, for convenience you may consider quilling somewhere between stick-lighting and needling. Of all the bird quills, the goose quill is the best kind, although it may be somewhat difficult to obtain. One place you might try is a live poultry market. If you get a fresh goose quill, be sure to leave the feathers in it. They seem to maintain some of the fat in the quill, which keeps it resilient and responsive for a long time. Plucking the feathers out will dry the quill rapidly and it won't work nearly as well. Unfortunately the feathers also keep the quill somewhat smelly for a couple of days, but after that time the smell dissipates.

Once the quill is ready to be used, the end should be cut on a bias. Holding the quill with the feathers bottom side up and the quill portion closest to you, take a sharp knife and place it perpendicular to the quill about ³/₄ of an inch from the end. Now, in a clockwise motion, cut around the quill moving your knifeblade forward on a slant. Make sure you have a sharp knife as some of the quills are quite tough. They are also a little slippery, so watch your fingers. The stem should be cut with one slice so that the end result looks like figure 15-9.

If you can get an entire goose wing and hang it in a corner somewhere, you will have a ready supply of quills as you need them. You can practice which degree of bias works best for you, and also have a number of quills around to get the effects you want. The moisture and oils within the wing will prevent the quills from becoming rapidly brittle.

The quill may be held with the concavity of the point either up or down. The amount of matt removed by the point and the type of line you will get depend on the amount of pressure you exert. This is where the resiliency of the quill is so important and plays such a large part in the effect. Of the three texturing tools we have mentioned, only the quill enables such flexibility within the line: both the stick-light and the needle have fixed points. Even more than the brush, the quill permits graded control of individual highlights, and when used together with the highlight brush, as in hair texturing, the effects can be stunning.

Incidentally, the undersides of the feathers can also be used in texturing. Make sure, if you are going to use your quill in this manner, that you clean the feathers well after use. Otherwise the matt will dry on them and make them brittle. The best way to get matt off the feathers is to let it dry and then just dust it off. Don't let it build up to any great extent, however, before you do this; damage occurs when layers of matt accumulate.

It is unfortunate that it is so difficult to obtain fresh quills. We have tried to find a reasonable substitute for them; the closest we have been able to come is a plastic tube cut in the same manner.

Fig. 15-9 The end of the quill should be cut in this fashion to get the best effects from it. The quill is seen from the underside.

Old-fashioned penpoints have also been substituted. You might find your own substitute for the goose quill. Generally speaking any substance that will provide that sort of resiliency together with a fine edge and point that will stand up under the exigencies of the work involved should do the trick. So far plastic seems to have the most promise.

Tracing over matt is a highly specialized technique, but it is one which you would do well to acquaint yourself with. It can be a great timesaver, especially if you are doing many pieces and want to get all your tracing and matting done at the same time. Even if you are only painting one piece of glass, it is well worth it if you

Tracing over Matt

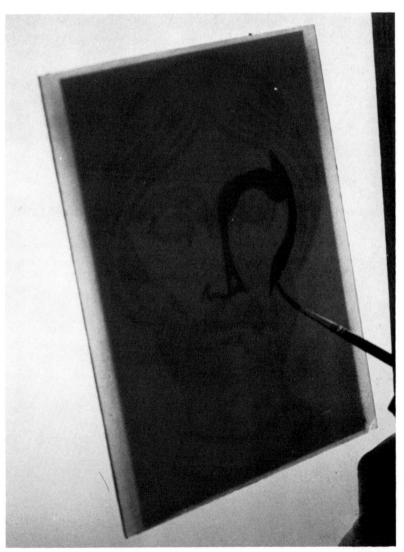

Fig. 15-10 When tracing over unfired matt, the brush strokes are a little more resistant and it is more difficult to see the cartoon. Here the unfired matt is holding up quite well under the trace line.

can save a firing. The process involves applying and blending a light matt, putting the matted glass over the cartoon, and using a vinegar trace (see chapter 7) directly over the unfired matt (figure 15-10). Obviously there is no room for error here. If you make a mistake in your tracing you will have to remove everything—not only all the trace, but all the matt as well, right down to the bare glass, and start over. Many painters find this factor makes the whole technique too inhibiting for them and don't use it at all. Others prefer tracing over matt to tracing on bare glass. We think it is good to be familiar with the process not only because it is something you can use, but also because the discipline involved is excellent training in tracing. Once you've gotten used to tracing over matt you will find "normal" tracing pretty much second nature.

In tracing over unfired matt, you will find a certain restraint to brush strokes you are used to accomplishing with a slip and a slide on glass alone. You will find it necessary to adapt your hand to this different "feel." Be very careful that you do not blob the trace paint. Don't overload your brush; make sure that your tracer is in the right position to do the best job. There is no possibility in this process of cleaning up sloppy trace lines with a stylus. What you trace is what you get. That is one of the reasons this technique is such a good discipline.

Here are a few suggestions applicable to this process:

1. Do not matt up your glass so heavily that you will barely be able to make out the cartoon when you go to trace.

2. Don't use so deep a color of glass that you can barely make

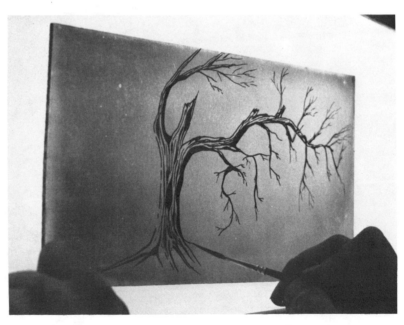

Fig. 15-11 Work in progress by Gary S. Ecker. A tree scene, with black trace over unfired matt. Here delicate lines are traced onto the tree.

Fig. 15-12 The completed tree, placed into an entire scene. If you look closely at the bottom branches you can see the name *STEVEN*. All work accomplished with trace, matt, and highlighting.

out the cartoon in its unmatted state. A cartoon is meant to be followed respectfully. To improve visibility, decrease surface reflective light and increase the light from the light table.

3. The matt should be well blended with as few irregularities in its surface as possible. It is much easier to move your tracer over a smooth surface and achieve a clean line than over a rough surface.

4. Wait to trace until you are certain the matt is completely dry. Don't be in such a hurry to try out the technique that you start to apply your tracer over wet matt.

5. Don't let the process overawe you. Keep practicing and eventually you will get it down. You should try to be as versatile as possible, utilizing all the medium of glass painting has to offer. Tracing over matt is not a procedure that is generally taught, or, indeed, generally considered, except in certain English studios. All the same it is one more basic technique which can serve to make you more flexible as a craftsman.

Aciding

Aciding (or etching), though not actually a painting activity, is involved intimately with it, and no book dealing with painting on glass would be complete without a brief review of this intriguing procedure. Aciding glass is the process of eating away portions that you do not want from the surface, leaving other areas standing out not only in bas-relief, but in a different color from the background. In a sense the effect can be compared to highlighting. The endeavor is made possible because hydrofluoric acid attacks the silica in the glass mixture. (Sandblasting glass, which gives a similar effect, is a different process entirely.) See the round windows in the color section for examples of etched stained glass.

Aciding is a simple enough procedure, providing you take a few precautions. Hydrofluoric acid will act on your skin, and it is possible to get burned very badly. Never handle glass during the acid-ing process without rubber gloves or tongs (you can buy them in a photographic supply store). Do not inhale the fumes from the acid. If you do not have a hood in your studio (and few of us do), it is best to work out of doors or in a very well-ventilated room. Do not use more of the acid than you need for the specific job, and pour it carefully from the storage container into the aciding tray (again the photographic supply store will come in handy here for a strong plastic tray).

When you dilute the acid (it comes full strength from stained glass or chemical supply houses) always add acid to water, never the other way round, as the acid has a greater density than the water. Occasionally we use the acid full strength, but rarely. The aciding process is quicker, but cruder, with full strength acid. The smoother mix is close to half and half, or even $1/3$ acid to $2/3$ water. Even in this diluted state, you must take precautions with the acid.

The method of preparing glass for aciding is as follows. Take a piece of flashed (two-color) glass and wrap it with clear contact paper. Keep in mind which is the flashed and which the "white" side. Only the flashed side will etch, of course, and if you forget which is which you can waste a lot of time waiting for the wrong side to develop out. With the contact paper firmly in place, take a sharp knife or razor blade and cut out the design that you wish to etch. Then put the glass into the acid bath using the tongs. Depending on the color, the thickness of the glass, and the strength of the acid bath you will shortly begin to see the etching process taking place. Etch away the color, but no more. There is little sense in going too deep as this will weaken the glass, and such areas of strain can crack in the firing process after the piece has been painted. Once the color has been removed, take the glass from the bath with the tongs and place it into a water bath which should be right near by. You don't want to walk across the room with the glass held only by the tongs. Swish the glass about in the water, wash off the tips of the tongs, lift the glass from the water bath with the tongs, and hold it under running water for several minutes. After this it should be safe to handle with your fingers. Peel away the contact paper and the etching process is completed. (To rapidly neutralize the acid, use ammonia.)

Hair Technique

The painting of hair so as to demonstrate its flow and flair seems to fill many students with dismay, but there is really nothing terribly difficult about it. The technique can be a combination of brush strokes and thick and thin quill work. Matting on the back side of the glass with lights removed with a long bristled highlight brush can also be done. This helps give a certain depth to the hair. Most of the graceful curve and fall of long hair is dependent on the strokes applied with your quill. Practice developing a "hair" stroke on a plain matted field; then combine that with a highlight brush in a way that you think best exemplifies the quality of the particu-

Fig. 15-13 Examples of hair technique from medieval windows.

lar kind of hair you wish to present. Thick, wavy tresses require more finger and wrist work, especially with the quill, than does straight hair. The idea is to take out the basic values with the highlight brush and accent some lines with the quill. Silver stain may be used arbitrarily on the other side of the glass to present blond highlights. The quill, more than the stylus, tends to provide a more natural flow to the highlight lines that are so much a part of good hair work.

Hair can also be traced. On our practice head the hair was traced as individual lines. When matt is applied over these trace lines, the hair may be highlighted with the quill to have a more natural effect. Try doing this highlighting several different ways. Try matting the piece of glass on the back and highlighting along the traced hair from this direction. After using the quill alone, use one of the long bristled highlight brushes alone. Then use the quill on top of the brush strokes. You may also want to utilize the technique of multiple matting for the hair. It is, you will find, very effective.

Study the hair styles of the heads presented in figure 15-13 and in the next chapter. In most cases trace, matt, and highlighting are combined to give an effect that is complimentary to the particular head that is portrayed.

CHAPTER 16

Head, Hair, and Drapery Examples

Three areas that most students and many advanced workers have trouble with are the painting of hair, head, and drapery. The following photographs provide several heads and figures for you to study and work with. Of course, the more you learn, the more subtle the difficulties you will encounter, and we can only do so much in these pages in the way of instruction. All the same, illustration and demonstration are invaluable teaching tools, and careful study of these examples should prove quite instructive. All the illustrations in this chapter are taken from *Religiöse Malereien für Kirchedekoration* by F. Eurban (Vienna: Anton Schroll, 1907).

Drapery

The figure on the left in figure 16-1 shows an interesting combination of cloth and skin textures, with a varying of brush stroke, stippling, and shadowing to achieve the effect. The drapery on the right figure has long vertical folds from bodice to ground with excess cloth crumpled at the foot. The widespread arms flare the cloak. Note how the wide sleeves are accomplished. Careful shadowing and highlighting are important elements in this representation. Imagine how flat the drapery would appear, how undimensional, without it.

Figure 16-2 is a study in long, almost unbroken vertical folds which are almost straight lines. The dots furnish a nice stacatto break for the eye amid all those long lines. If the lines were more curvaceous, the dots would make the pattern too busy. Imagine these dots in the other drapery examples shown; the effect would be dizzying. Even here, the dots are kept to less than half the surface—enough for a variation on what would otherwise be a monotous flow of line, but not enough to be confusing. Also providing variation in those long folds is the matting, used as shadow in discrete areas.

Almost the exact opposite to figure 16-2, figure 16-3 shows a wildly flowing line of drapery, the curves and folds doubling on themselves. Extensive use of matt provides the dimensional shadowing. This figure demonstrates how ornate an essentially simple drapery can become just from the billows of the cloth itself. No embroidery is needed to garnish this decor; it has achieved a rich lamination from its own tucks and sweeps.

201

Fig. 16-1 Two drapery examples.

Fig. 16-2 Repeated vertical folds enhanced by shadowing and dots.

Fig. 16-3 Billowing drapery needs little else for dramatic effect.

Fig. 16-4 Elaborately decorated fabric combined with graceful folds.

In both examples in figure 16-4, the drapery is not only rich in folds but in embroidered design as well. Contrast these figures with 16-3. Here the figures are static; the cloth is not in motion. There is motion enough with all that brilliant inlay. We have seen how folds of cloth alone can be demonstrative when provided with flow; here the emphasis is on the impressed rather than the expressed design. The folds are important, but secondary to the fabric itself, which bespeaks a quieter, albeit ponderous, dignity. Painting drapery is not just a matter of indicating a few folds here and there. It is a matter of utilizing the drapery to express the tenor of a scene. And it is all done with trace and matt.

Heads

The head in figure 16-5 is a sketchy fill-in of the features with trace; you can almost get away without using any matting on the proper flesh-toned glass. Note the wisps of hair, the brief lines of trace that indicate features. Note also the stippling of the matt over the far side of the face.

In figure 16-6 trace lines are used much more definitively than in 16-5. The features are more strongly realized, which takes much of the mystery out of this face compared to the face in 16-5. These are two totally different techniques you should be acquainted with.

The heads in figures 16-7 and 16-8 are almost the same face, seen from different angles. While the technique of matting and tracing remain the same, perspective changes. This, in turn, influences how the trace and matt will be applied.

Head 16-7 is a three-quarter view without highlighting. It is a good example of the relationship of features to one another at this particular tilt of the head. Matting is minimum. You might like to try adding your own shadowing to this basic outline. Remember the light is coming from over your left shoulder.

16-8 is a full face with a minimum of highlighting. There is some shadowing in the cloak. Again we see the relationship of the facial features, especially of the chin to the line of the neck. All of these are trace lines. This is a good example for matting and highlighting practice.

The faces in figures 16-9 and 16-10 are both three-quarter views. We chose one male and one female face to demonstrate the facial differences as manifested in the trace lines. Almost all of this is linear detail. As in the other examples, matting is minimal. In the male face, the eyebrows, nose line, and lips are usually the most forceful characteristics. Trace lines are more delicate and the features are finer in the female. These are elements to take into consideration when painting heads. Such characteristics would, of course, be placed into your original cartoon, but they must be carried out further in your trace lines as well. It is important to get experience in tracing both male and female heads.

Hair

In figure 16-11 the hair is lightly indicated by short trace lines within a matted area. The eye is guided by these hints to assume

Fig. 16-5 Stippling and sketchy trace lines impart a sense of mystery to the face.

Fig. 16-6 Features are well drawn, but the tracing lacks character.

Fig. 16-7 Good example of perspective. Minimal highlighting, though, and little character to the trace lines.

Fig. 16-8 Another test of perspective.

Fig. 16-9 Eyes and lips are indicated with fine trace lines and delicate shading.

Fig. 16-10 Brow, nose, and lips are frequently dominant features in the male face.

Fig. 16-11 Texture of hair is effectively suggested by a minimum of line and shading.

Fig. 16-12 Hair is forcefully represented, with greater use of trace and matt than in the previous example.

Fig. 16-13 A minimum of trace and shading subtly indicates the facial hair and beard.

Fig. 16-14 Extensive, fine detailing impart an extraordinary realism to this head.

Fig. 16-15 A formal hairdo.

Fig. 16-16 A more casual hairdo.

Fig. 16-17 A tonsure indicated by trace lines.

Fig. 16-18 A tonsure indicated with trace lines and matt.

Fig. 16-19 Twisty trace lines activate an otherwise formal hairdo.

Fig. 16-20 Flowing but carefully contained lines in the hair emphasize the placidness of this head.

the hair texture. Note how the part of the hair is subtly indicated. Matting and highlighting are very important in providing substance to the illusion created by the trace lines.

In 16-12 the hair is more specific, and the scalp is quite filled in with trace lines. These two could almost be the same head, with the light hitting the hair from different angles. The dominance of the head in 16-12 is provided by the hair. In 16-11 the eyes dominate the face, and the hair is subdued in comparison.

The same sort of technique is used in figures 16-13 and 16-14 as in the previous examples, but this time with a beard. In 16-13 the beard is simply indicated by an outline and a few minimal trace lines to furnish substance. There really is no hair, per se, shown. In 16-14, however, it is a different story. Here the hair is specifically demonstrated; one can almost reach out and fluff the whiskers. Note the curling of the hair done with brush, stick-light, and quill so that we can actually see individual strands. Which is the better painting? Neither. They provide two different, conclusive effects. Both are legitimate. You should practice both techniques.

Figure 16-15 shows a pretty formal hairdo, rigid within the lead lines that encompass it. The trace lines follow a strict sort of swirl, fairly uniform. No stray strand escapes, as expected—it is that sort of head. But look now at 16-16, how almost windblown, in comparison, is the hair. It looks much less formal; in fact it gives the impression of flowing all about. Yet it is just as tightly bounded by its lead line as the hair in 16-15. All the action is taking place within the lead lines, imparted by the trace lines, and mainly by those going foreward onto the forehead. It is this out of place swirl that gives the impression of waywardness. Take that away and the hair would be pretty nearly as formally set as in the head above. It doesn't take a whole lot of emphasis to make a point.

The tonsure is yet another hair style as seen in figures 16-17 and 16-18. In the side view we see how the curls of hair, represented by trace lines, provide a fringe through their individual shapes. This fringe can be left alone or, as in figure 16-18, augmented with matt to give the fringe even more dimension. In both instances note how the hair is allowed to tuck under the ear, as it would normally do.

The two formal hair styles in figures 16-19 and 16-20 have decidedly different tones. In 16-19, the hair is in braids but the face is in knots. The set of eyes, nose, and mouth indicates anger, if not rage. The hair somewhat contributes to this wildness—the trace lines indicate some shaking of the hair—but the formal pattern remains. The hair is not sticking up all over the place just because the face is angry. In 16-20, face and hair are placid. Note the difference in the trace line patterns. In 16-20 they are all curves and softness; in 16-19 a twistiness to the lines gives the braids an impression of cavorting. It doesn't take much to give a completely different effect.

✥ CHAPTER 17

Silver Staining

The staining process has a marked fascination for beginning glass painters. There is a particularly anticipatory air in class when stained pieces are due to come out of a kiln. This is because with stain you never can be sure just what you will get as an effect until the cooled piece of glass is actually in your hand. Then you may experience either disappointment or triumph. Even the disappointments, however, are dramatic.

The basic effect of silver stain is to turn the glass yellow. All shades of yellow are possible, from a faint straw tinge to a deep golden color, depending on such factors as type of glass, amount of stain, and firing temperature. Silver stain may be used on clear glass to obtain a variety of rich and subtle effects. But glass need not be clear to show a stain effect well. You can get very interesting variations of hue by combining silver stain with colored glass.

Another way to use stain, one which can provide a triple-hue arrangement, is to acid out (etch) portions of a flashed glass to the underlying color and apply stain to some of these etched areas. With a flashed blue on clear, you can, in the same piece of glass, have a blue color, a blue/white from the etched but unstained portions, plus green from the stain over pale blue.

One effect of stain is to save a lead line, to color in a section of the work that otherwise would require a separate piece of yellow glass. Often such an area (a halo, for instance) might be uncuttable for a single piece of glass, or even two, thus adding awkward lead lines and spoiling the design. So staining is a practical as well as an aesthetic tool. Many workers feel that if they are using stain they have to stain everything in sight, especially if aciding is involved. But this is rarely a wise course. It is not only possible to be discriminate in applying stain, it is often far more aesthetic to leave something alone to provide a particular effect, rather than cover it with stain simply because you have the stain brush in your hand. One such discriminate effect can be obtained by staining around the edges of an acided area, leaving the central portion clear. This will give a nice halo effect.

Staining is a technique in its own right and not just a way of poking color around on the back of a piece of glass to achieve drama of questionable value or to distract the eye from inferior painting in the foreground. Either of these reasons are too often the impetus for using stain. The staining effect should be used discriminately, not overdone or used haphazardly.

211

How Silver Stain Works

By itself silver nitrate stain is colorless, but what you buy comes as a brownish-red powder. This powder is a nonfiring pigment which has several purposes. For one thing, it helps the worker know how thick he is applying the stain, since it would be very difficult to do so with a colorless substance. Secondly, it helps stabilize the silver nitrate, providing it with an even, effective firing range. In point of fact, silver nitrate, which is the basic stain substance, is not a very good stain by itself. It tends to melt erratically, and under these circumstances it is next to impossible to predict what kind of stain it will leave and what its intensity will be. Other silver salts added to the silver nitrate help alleviate this problem. Other chemicals in the brownish powder act almost like a sponge, pulling certain elements out of the glass and allowing the silver to take their place. This is why silver nitrate is a stain—it actually penetrates the glass and becomes part of its structure.

When you paint your silver stain onto the surface of a piece of glass and heat it, you are putting into motion a complex process. Glass is composed of an irregular network of silica and boric oxide, and this network has empty spaces within which other elements fit, depending on the type of glass. In the kind of glass we're considering, one of those elements is sodium. The silver in the stain is also the right atomic size to fit into one of these network "holes." In order to do so, it has to push out whatever element happens to be occupying that space—namely the sodium. Sodium comes out, silver comes in. What happens to this displaced sodium? Certain chemical reactions occurring in the brown mixture hold onto it. The more sodium in the glass, the easier it comes out, the better the glass takes the stain.

When the silver replaces the sodium in the glass network, the silver changes the light transmission of the glass. It now allows yellow light to pass through it but absorbs the rest of the spectrum, so what you see when you look at this glass is basically a yellow color. In this respect silver nitrate is a true stain, not a paint. The phenomenon is not only a surface modification, as is the case with paint. Glass stained with silver nitrate is permanently transformed throughout its substance.

Predicting the Stain Effect

The way your stain will look after firing depends on several factors. First is the amount of stain you apply. Transparency as well as depth will vary with the thickness of this "wash." A second factor is length of firing time. The intensity tends to become more pronounced as the firing time is increased, or as the temperature is raised over a constant time. A third factor is the kind of glass you are using. Some glasses take stain badly, others not at all. Last, the quality of the stain mixture that you are using certainly plays its part in the final effect. It is the combination of all of these variables that makes the staining process so tricky—and so challenging. No wonder students wait so avidly for that kiln to cool and the pieces to come out.

The only way to really predict the outcome of your silver staining efforts is to do some test firings of various dilutions of stain on various glasses and at various temperatures. Keep a record of your tests, otherwise you cannot hope to recreate the effects you want.

Certain glasses such as Pyrex have a very tight, bound-in network of atoms, and they are almost impossible to stain because the chemical network is so tight. In fact, the ordinary silver nitrate will not touch them. We mention this only to show how specialized each type of glass is as far as its ability to take stain is concerned. Today there are more glass manufacturers around than ever before producing all varieties and types of glass, and it is almost impossible to find a specific stain that will work equally on each specimen. If you intend to do any great amount of staining, inquire of the company you get your glass from how individual sheets take stain. If they don't know, you would be wise to test stain a sample. It might not stain at all, or the best you might be able to get is a faint amber color. Better to know before you purchase several cases. And just because one type of glass takes stain well, it doesn't mean all other types will, even though they are from the same company.

The best kind of glass to take stain is window glass. It is almost impossible, in most instances, for it not to soak in and stain a lovely yellow. But if you stumble onto a piece of window glass that has a slight tint for one reason or another, this tint can make the glass completely reject the stain or give it a blotchy, irregular appearance. The same is true of stained glass; even more so since stained glass has a great many chemicals added to it, any one of which can dislocate its staining properties. Selenium is one such material, used as a decolorizer in the glass staining process at the factory. Selenium will prevent a piece of glass from taking stain.

Sometimes glass will take stain better on one side than the other, as in flashed glass where it is often debatable whether the white side or the flashed side will stain best. You should take samples from the flashed glass you intend to stain to see the effects of stain on various color combinations. Obviously the flash-yellow will not be the one to try, but all the other colors, as well as flash-clear, are worth the experiment.

You must also experiment with dilutions of stain so you will know what shade of this brown/orange color will correspond to the color of yellow stain you want to achieve. When we test stain, we always try several dilutions, brush them on a piece of glass, perhaps even blend them on a clear piece of window glass, and then fire these experimental strokes after marking them (see color section). Only then can we tell which intensity of stain will best serve for the job in hand. There is a very slight difference in intensity between fired and unfired matt, but it seems to be one of character rather than tone. With unfired stain, however, the brown pigment as well as the clear nature of the stain itself obscures the color you will obtain after firing.

Another factor of stain effect is firing temperature. If the temperature in the kiln gets too hot, instead of getting a nice clear stain, you will find that your stained area has, when reflecting light, a sort of bluish-white halo effect. This may not be objectionable when you are looking *through* the glass, which is how stained glass is usually viewed, but when you gaze at it from an angle, this milky film can be visible. Any appearance of this bluish halo indicates over-firing.

Purchasing Stain

In the Reusche catalog are several stains which many beginners puzzle over. The usual question we get asked is, "Which is the best one for me to buy?" There are four in the catalog: 1382 Silver Stain Orange 1, 1383 Silver Stain Orange 2, 1384 Silver Stain Yellow 3, and 1388 Silver Stain Orange Intense. Oranges 1 and 2 are basically the same. Number 3 is a deep yellow. The fourth, the intense orange stain, is probably the best for the money since you can, by diluting it, make most of the other stain values from it. One way to do this is to put it very thinly on the glass to get hues lighter in shade than the actual intense color would provide. A greater range of values is available with deeper colors than lighter, and this one can go deep orange if you apply it heavily, or one of the yellow varieties if you put it on more thinly.

As for how much to buy at one time, this depends on how much you will use over how long a period of time. Stain does not go bad. We have kept stain for years, then trotted it out, used it, and put it away again. We saw no ill effects in the work from the stain not being "fresh." Silver stain does not have to be kept in dark bottles when it is being stored. Nor is there a problem in leaving the stain on your stain palette as long as you like. Don't rinse off your stain palette and flush this expensive chemical down the sink. We have reused stain left on a palette as long as eight months. The stain was still good. All you need do when you are ready to reuse your stain is to pour some vinegar over it and use your spatula to bring it back to the proper consistency.

Mixing Stain

Keep a special palette for your stains, as you have done with your various traces and matts, labeling the palette as well as the palette box. The brown powder that will come out of your silver stain packet is mixed pretty much in the same fashion as is trace or matt. A pile of stain is poured on the palette, a small hole is made in the center, and the vehicle is poured in. In the case of stain, the preferred vehicle is white vinegar because it allows the stain to distribute better in the mix, and the result is a smoother, more even flow over the glass. If you can't tolerate the smell of vinegar and are using water instead, be sure to mix the water and stain well with your spatula. Vinegar tends to go "flat" after a while, at least as a vehicle for trace or stain, and you can tell this by its resistance to affecting a proper blend when you are mixing it. Very often fresh vinegar will solve this problem rapidly.

It is not necessary to use any gum arabic with stain because it has all the "bite" it needs to take hold on the glass. If you use gum arabic you will make the stain practically unremovable from the glass even before it is fired, and you won't be able to work it to the desired effect.

The mixing process is just like mixing trace or matt. It is a good idea to keep a special spatula to mix your stain, one that you use to mix nothing else. It should be absolutely clean, because any dirt from the spatula will go quite readily into the stain. You will notice that after employing your palette knife on stain for awhile, it will start to get permanently discolored from the stain. However, this discoloration will not affect the stain and you may continue to use the palette knife so long as you are sure there is no other dirt or grime on top of this. A palette knife should always be rinsed off before working on any color, not just stain.

Keep in mind that the palette knife is constantly being honed against the glass palette and eventually a razor edge will develop. It is not a good idea, therefore, to run your fingers down its sides to see just how sharp the thing has gotten. For some reason this seems to be a constant temptation.

Some glass painters add a material called bluestone to their stain mix to get an even deeper color. It is a rather tricky business and we don't recommend doing it routinely. The bluestone must be ground in very well. If you add too much bluestone you are liable to make your color more rusty looking, a sort of beer bottle brown. You will also tend to get more of that bluish surface halation we spoke of earlier when you use bluestone in excess. When you add bluestone you are modifying the basic silver stain formula and, while there is the possibility you may make it better, there is always the chance you might make it worse and end up with a mess. It is one more variable in what is basically an unpredictable substance to begin with. However, if nothing else achieves the color you want, it is certainly worth a try.

Applying the Stain

When applying stain, do not put it on in a straight line, tracing fashion, but spread it over the area of the glass you wish to stain more or less like a matt. It can be just pushed about, it can be blended, or it can be worked however you wish with a variety of brushes. It doesn't take a special brush to apply stain. The best kind of brush for applying staining is any soft sort of brush, one that is thick and will spread nicely. Any brush you can use for matting or tracing can be used for staining, and you can utilize your tracers if you want a special effect. Keep a separate, cheap badger blender on hand for blending stain. We do advise that once you use a brush for staining you use it for nothing else as the feel of these brushes will begin to change and their bristles will begin to stiffen and drop out. You shouldn't, therefore, use a very good brush for staining. If you happen to pick up and use one by accident, make sure you wash it out right away with plenty of water, including the ferrule.

Staining brushes tend not to last too long; the quality of stain leads to an early death. You can extend the life of your staining brush by washing it *thoroughly* after use. Be careful—stain (as well as matt or trace) tends to accumulate at the ferrule, and stain left there will destroy the bristles. We strongly advise marking your brushes to indicate what they are being used for. The ideal, if you can afford it, is to have three sets of brushes: one for trace and matt, one for stain, and the third for oil (if you are going to be using any of the oil techniques). You needn't worry about mixing your water and vinegar brushes; these can be used interchangeably.

Stain is usually applied to the back portion of the glass where it forms a yellow substrait to the painted front surface. Since stain actually penetrates the glass, not merely covers a surface, it is equally effective from either side. Using it on the back is, therefore, a matter of convenience.

When you first paint your stain onto the glass, you will find a certain amount of "drag" to the brush. Unlike trace, stain does not flow readily. The drag effect is interesting as it tends to provide a certain measure of control—the brush doesn't slip over the glass. All you will see, of course, as you apply your stain is the brownish color due to the nonfiring pigment. The true yellow color that you want will not appear until after firing.

Firing Stained Pieces

Years ago most studios routinely had two separate firings—one for the trace/matt combination (however many that took) and one specifically for the stain. Many studios and many individual workers still adhere to this routine. Usually stain fires on window glass at about 1025° to 1050°F, whereas paint can fire as much as 100° higher. You can, if you wish, fire separately for stain, and in some instances it might be wise to do just this. However many workers, ourselves included, generally use one firing for both. You can compensate for the higher temperature by putting on a slightly more diluted stain. A lot depends on how special is the effect that you are after. If you are putting stain on very, very heavy for some particular endeavor, you might be better off to fire the stain after everything else so that you can fire at a lower temperature, depending on what you want the stain to look like. You will have to experiment to work out the correct firing temperature for the particular job in hand.

If you are going to fire stain and paint in a single firing, always fire the stain side of the glass down against the kiln shelf (prepared with kiln wash). The paint, of course, is then fired up, facing the elements of the kiln. This is strictly a practical matter. It is not that stain fires best in this "down" position. It is done because the stain will not stick to the kiln wash or the shelf, and the paint just might—which would be a disaster. In point of fact, stain fires equally well up or down.

Firing paint and stain together usually presents no basic problems provided you don't go too high with the kiln temperature. Up to 1175°F or even a bit over 1200°F is still safe. Above that, the stain will start to develop a dark, rusty color and may even go blotchy. Once the temperature has reached what you consider the proper level, the kiln is shut off and allowed to cool. As discussed in chapter 6, all painted or stained pieces should not be removed from the kiln until they are cool to warm.

Once you do remove it, you still won't be able to tell how your stain has fired because the brownish pigment will still be there. Take a moist rag and wipe this away. Like magic, you will find beneath the glorious yellow color you have hoped for. With luck.

Occasionally there are problems with the brown pigment. It sometimes sticks onto the glass after firing is completed, giving a blotchy effect which you will not be able to remove. We've seen this happen to individuals who certainly didn't deserve it, having observed all the staining and firing rules. Chances are that if you get these ugly brown blotches you have fired too high for the specific type of glass you are using. An over-firing of this nature can result in an actual fusing of the brown pigment into the glass surface. As we have warned, it is most important to test fire your glass to see how it reacts to stain and modify the temperature accordingly. In staining, particularly, temperature is a critical factor.

At the same time, you may go through all sorts of contortions to make absolutely certain each step is precise and still end up with stain that doesn't take or "nonfiring" pigment that does. In this case it could be the fault of the stain. The nonfiring pigment (iron oxide) that is mixed in with the silver stain is a bit quixotic. For instance, sometimes Venetian Red, a type of iron oxide, is mixed with a certain quantity of lime to make it work better. Unfortunately if too much lime gets into the mix it can "poison" the stain and prevent the reaction from occurring. So, if all else fails and your stain is still not working, you might call the manufacturer and tell him. He might have something else for you to try, or he might replace your batch with a fresh one. You've nothing to lose by calling him; most manufacturers of stained glass supplies are eager to keep their customers happy.

Few things in painting are so gratifying as wiping away the brown pigment and seeing the golden stained area appear for the first time. As often as we have done it, we still cannot deny the thrill that comes when a stained area works out just right. When it doesn't, well, you have the excitement of doing the thing better the next time.

Substituting Enamel for Stain

Because of the tricky nature of stain, some painters have attempted to substitute yellow enamel for the stain. However, yellow enamel is not the same thing as stain. We feel that enamel paints certainly have their place, but to use an enamel rather than a glass-painting color simply as a matter of convenience is self-deceiving.

All those transparent enamel colors are very soft paints with low-firing temperatures; they are not very resistant and will end up fading in a comparatively short time. And the truth of the matter is that in the long run it is probably easier to use stain than to use enamels. More fun, too. One exception that we can think of to the general transitory nature of enamel paints are those enamels used like stain in the fifteenth-century Swiss heraldic panels. These paints do have a great deal of depth, are very dense and give almost the impression of a piece of flashed glass when you look at them. However these types of colors don't seem to be made today—certainly they are not in the usual catalogs.

BIBLIOGRAPHY AND SUGGESTED READING

Many of the richest resources for style, design, and inspiration in stained glass painting are older books no longer readily available. Nevertheless, listing some of them here may give you an idea of what to look for. A search of nearby libraries and antiquary book stores should yield a few volumes that will be useful to you.

Connick, Charles. *Adventures in Light and Color*. New York: Harrap and Co., Ltd. 1937.

Day, Lewis F. *Windows: A Book about Stained and Painted Glass*. New York: B. T. Batsford. 1909.

Delamotte, F. G. *Medieval Alphabets and Initials for Illuminators*. London: J. Willis Brooks. 1861.

Drake, Maurice. *A History of English Glass Painting*. Clifford's Inn, London: T. Werner Laurie, Ltd. 1912.

Hancock, E. Campbell. *The Amateur Pottery and Glass Painter*. London: Chapman and Hall. 1920.

Harrison, F. *The Painted Glass of York*. New York: Macmillan. 1927.

Isenberg, Anita, and Isenberg, Seymour. *How to Work in Stained Glass*. Radnor, Pa.: Chilton Book Co. 1972.

————. *Stained Glass: Advanced Techniques and Projects*. Radnor, Pa.: Chilton Book Co. 1976.

Knowles, John. *Essays in the History of the York School of Glasspainting*. London: Macmillan Co. 1936.

Lee, Lawrence. *The Appreciation of Stained Glass*. London: Oxford University Press. 1977.

Lee, Lawrence; Seddon, George; and Stephens, Francis. *Stained Glass*. New York: Crown. 1976.

Lowe, J. *Handbook of Porcelain and Glass*. London: Longman's, Greene. 1862.

Lubke, Wilhelm. *Ecclesiastical Art in Germany during the Middle Ages*. London: Thos. Jack Co. 1870.

Nelson, Philip. *Ancient Painted Glass in England 1170–1500*. London: Methuen and Co. 1913.

Norman, Barbara. *Engraving and Decorating Glass*. New York: McGraw-Hill. 1972.

Racinet, A. C. *Handbook of Ornaments in Color*. New York: Van Nostrand Reinhold.

Reyntiens, Patrick. *The Technique of Stained Glass*. New York: Watson-Guptill. 1967.

Saint, Lawrence, and Arnold, Hugh. *Stained Glass of the Middle Ages in England and France*. London: A. and C. Black. 1913.

Sharpe, Edmund. *Decorated Windows*. London: John Voorst. 1909.

Sowers, Robert. *The Lost Art*. New York: George Wittenborn, Inc. 1954.

————. *Stained Glass: An Architectural Art*. New York: Universe Books. 1965.

Twining, E. W. *The Art and Craft of Stained Glass*. London: Pitman and Sons. 1928.

Wallace-Dunlop, M. A. *Glass in the Old World*. London: Field and Co. 1921.

Werck, Alfred. *Stained Glass: A Handbook*. New York: Adelphi Co. 1926.

Whall, C. W. *Stained Glass Work*. London: John Hogg. 1905.

Winston. *An Inquiry into the Difference of Style Observable in Ancient Glass Painting*. London: Oxford University Press. 1887.

Woodforde, Christopher. *The Norwich School of Glass-Painting in the Fifteenth Century*. London: Oxford University Press. 1950.

SOURCES OF SUPPLY

The following list is not meant to be exhaustive. Check your yellow pages and local hobby and craft stores first—there may be a source of stained glass supplies in your area. Not all stained glass suppliers will have brushes and paints, however. The major supplier of these is L. Reusche and Co. of Newark, NJ.

There are many manufacturers of small ceramic or enameling kilns appropriate for firing glass. These kilns can be purchased from or through local ceramic studios or ceramic hobby stores. Be sure to comparison shop and to get a kiln with the features you need. If you get involved in a big way and want a flash kiln, contact L. Reusche and Co.

Nervo Distributors
650 University Ave.
Berkeley, CA 94710

C. and R. Loo
1550 62nd St.
Emeryville, CA 94662

Hollander Glass, Inc.
2939 East Anaheim St.
Long Beach, CA 90804

Stained Glass & Supplies, Inc.
2104 Colorado Blvd.
Los Angeles, CA 90041

New Renaissance Glass
Works
5151 Broadway
Oakland, CA 94611

Stained Glass Forest
2312 K St.
Sacramento, CA 95816

Yesterday's Glass
110 West Colonial Drive
Orlando, FL 32801

Dorothy's Stained Glass
Studio
903 North Orchard
Boise, ID 83704

Art Glass of Illinois
105 Oakwood Park
East Peoria, IL 61611

Sunrise Art Glass Studios
1113 Chicago Ave.
Oak Park, IL 60302

Stained Glass Caboose
6102 Springwood Court
Baltimore, MD 21206

Vortex Stained Glass Studio
Main Street
West Stockbridge, MA
01266

Delphi Craft Supply Center
2224 East Michigan Ave.
Lansing, MI 48912

Gaytee Stained Glass
2744 Lyndale Ave. South
Minneapolis, MN 55408

Glass House Studio, Inc.
125 State St.
St. Paul, MN 55107

Boesen's Glasscraft, Inc.
2203 North 91st Plaza
Omaha, NE 68134

The Stained Glass Club
PO Box 244
Norwood, NJ 07648

Endeavor Products, Ltd.
443 East First Ave.
Roselle, NJ 07203

Glass Masters, Inc.
154 West 18th St.
New York, NY 10010

S. A. Bendheim Co.
122 Hudson Street
New York, NY 10013

Franklin Glass Art Studio
222 East Sycamore St.
Columbus, OH 43206

Pendleton Studios
3895 North Tulsa Ave.
Oklahoma City, OK 73112

Cline Glass Co., Inc.
1135 SE Grand Ave.
Portland, OR 97214

Glass Haus Studio
1819 South Alameda
Corpus Christi, TX 78404

Village Hobby Mart
  2414 Bolsover
  Houston, TX 77005

Black's Art Glass
  3225 North Flores
  San Antonio, TX 78212

Tiffany Touch
  337 West 21st St.
  Norfolk, VA 23517

Northwest Art Glass
  904 Elliott Ave. West
  Seattle, WA 98117

Ed Hoy's Stained Glass
  999 East Chicago Ave.
  Naperville, IL 60540

Tiffany Stained Glass Ltd.
  549 North Wells St.
  Chicago, IL 60610

The Stained Glass Shoppe
  2315 North 45th St.
  Seattle, WA 98103

Stained Glass Studio
  1232 East Brady St.
  Milwaukee, WI 53202

PAINTING SUPPLIES
L. Reusche & Co.
  2–6 Lister Avenue
  Newark, NJ 07105

INDEX